The Healing Power of WATER

○○○

Please visit Hay House USA: www.hayhouse.com®
Hay House Australia: www.hayhouse.com.au
Hay House UK: www.hayhouse.co.uk
Hay House South Africa: www.hayhouse.co.za
Hay House India: www.hayhouse.co.in

The Healing
Power of
WATER

Masaru Emoto

Consultant Editor: Elizabeth Puttick

Hay House, Inc.
Carlsbad, California • New York City
London • Sydney • Johannesburg
Vancouver • Hong Kong • New Delhi

Published and distributed in the United States by: Hay House, Inc.: www.hayhouse.
com • *Published and distributed in Australia by:* Hay House Australia Pty. Ltd.:
www.hayhouse.com.au • *Published and distributed in the United Kingdom by:*
Hay House UK, Ltd.: www.hayhouse.co.uk • *Published and distributed in the
Republic of South Africa by:* Hay House SA (Pty), Ltd.: www.hayhouse.co.za •
Distributed in Canada by: Raincoast: www.raincoast.com • *Published in India
by:* Hay House Publishers India: www.hayhouse.co.in

Original German publication *(Die Heilkraft des Wassers),* 2004 by Koha-Verlag
GmbH Burgrain, Germany

Translated by: Sonia Aichi and Ines Rusteberg • *Design:* Amy Gingery

Photography from IHM Research Institute: Takashige Kizu, Seiko Ikeda, Hiroshi Oida,
Takayuki Oshide, Takeshi Katsumata, Jun Futamura, Kouji Sakamoto, Masaya Sato,
Migiwa Tanaka / *Photographs from Amana Images:* © Tsutomu Takasaki; © kanehisa
Murakami; © Cross wave; © MasatoTokiwa; © Fumio Okita

Library of Congress Cataloging-in-Publication Data

Heilkraft des Wassers . English.
  The healing power of water / [edited by] Masaru Emoto ; consultant editor,
Elizabeth Puttick. -- 1st ed.
    p. cm.
  ISBN 978-1-4019-0876-8 (hardcover) -- ISBN 978-1-4019-0877-5 (tradepaper) 1.
Water--Therapeutic use. 2. Water--Religious aspects. 3. Water--Experiments. I.
Emoto, Masaru, 1943- II. Puttick, Elizabeth, 1952- III. Title.
  RA591.5.H4513 2007
  613.2'87--dc22
                            2007001835

Hardcover ISBN: 978-1-4019-0876-8
Tradepaper ISBN: 978-1-4019-0877-5

10 09 08 07   5 4 3 2
1st Hay House edition, September 2007
2nd edition, October 2007

Printed in Singapore

CONTENTS

PART III: SPIRITUAL AND MYTHOLOGICAL PERSPECTIVES

Foreword

S o many people all over the world have been touched and impressed by the research and findings of the work of Dr. Masaru Emoto. His groundbreaking first book, *The Message from Water,* awakened us to the simple but profound connection between our thoughts and the effect they have not only on our own bodies, but on water itself. Wow! What a novel idea.

This information gave me a new respect for water. I began blessing with love every glass of water I drank. Labels appeared on my faucets, showerhead, garden watering cans, the toilets, every other water source I had, and all the many bottles of water I carried everywhere.

I heard more and more from others who were using Dr. Emoto's information to expand and change their own work to include respect for water. It was only a natural progression to gather this information into a book to share with the world.

Dr. Emoto has taken all that he knows about the magic of water and utilized the current brilliant minds of people from the scientific, health, and spiritual worlds, combined with the mythological realms, to give you the most comprehensive study of water and its powers. Personally, I think *The Healing Power of Water* may be his best work to date. If you want to know, for instance, the myths of water (such as the healing power of the waters at Lourdes), you can read that section of the book. You can also discover what scientists say comprises the structure of water. For me, I jumped right to the information pertaining to health. How often have we heard the advice to drink eight glasses of water a day? These chapters delve deeper into the questions of water and its power to heal.

Dr. Emoto and I have visited with each other on a number of occasions, most recently at my 80th birthday party. At that lovely celebration, he presented me with a beautifully framed photograph of a magnificent water crystal, which had been formed out of the words *You can heal your life*. It brought tears of joy to my eyes to see what a beautiful water crystal looked like based on the title of my best-selling book. I've always believed in the healing power of words, and this very learned gentleman presented this very simple lady with a precious gift. I will treasure it always.

You have in your hands Masaru Emoto's latest endeavor, *The Healing Power of Water*, and it's my honor to be writing this Foreword. Dr. Emoto's work has sparked a revolution! It's heartening to have so many authors studying and sharing their thoughts about the healing power of water. I hope you find what you are looking for in these pages.

— **Louise L. Hay**

✿✿✿ ✿✿✿

You can heal your life crystal.

INTRODUCTION

I first had the idea of freezing water and photographing the crystals thus formed in 1994. Since then, several books have come out on my work, featuring both visual images of water crystals and the insights that I've gained from my research. These volumes have been translated into many languages, and I regularly travel all over the world to give lectures about my experiences with water. And every time, I'm touched anew by how people can *intuitively* relate to the images of the water crystals.

For both my colleagues and myself, this last decade has involved years of intensive development and research. Although the technique of water-crystal photography has to be further refined to meet the strict demands of the scientific community, it's inspiring to witness the interest with which the pictures are examined and the immediate understanding of their meaning at a lay level. We hope that you, too, will gain a new awareness of the wonderful and miraculous world of water.

Masaru Emoto

WATER: THE HEALER IN US

Why are we so fascinated by water? Since the beginning of time, it has been seen as a symbol of the soul and regarded as the *prima materia,* the prime substance, of the universe. Life itself developed out of the sea, the human fetus is surrounded and protected by the amniotic fluid, and our body consists of at least 70 percent water—the examples could go on and on.

Water as a physical substance possesses some of the features that made life possible on Earth. We all learned about its anomalies in our physics classes. For instance, frozen water is lighter than the liquid. Without this quality, rivers would freeze completely from top to bottom in winter; but because a lighter, protective layer of ice forms on the surface, creatures can still exist underneath.

Water also has the ability to levitate. It can flow against gravity, as in the case of artesian springs and wells. The healing power of water from these sources, for both external and internal use, has been known for generations.

In my book *Die Antwort des Wassers* (*Water Knows the Answer*), I described the amazing journey of one drop of water. I'd like to look at this journey once again, but from a different point of view, using it as an analogy for human life.

EVERYTHING IS IN A STATE OF CHANGE

In Buddhism and Shintoism, two religions that have significantly influenced our way of thinking in Japan, reincarnation is an absolutely integral component. This idea of cyclic development, of spiraling, corresponds well with the journey of a drop of water. A drop might start its journey as water, then evaporate, changing its form. It's still water, but it's not the same as before. However, the same knowledge, the same information, is still there. The same applies even when it's frozen.

I would say that the process of evaporating is equivalent to dying. Then we, too, change our shape, our form. The body dissolves, but the information that the soul has acquired—all the experiences and everything that we've learned—is maintained. Now the soul sets out on its own journey. It develops further and matures until it's time for it to incarnate again on Earth—just as the water drop rises as steam, falls back as a raindrop out of a cloud, trickles away into the earth, and after a very long time (100 to 1,000 years), appears again on the surface of the earth as an artesian spring.

We don't know exactly what processes a drop of water goes through inside the earth before the astonishing power of levitation finally sets in and it rises up hundreds of feet. But we do know that artesian springs have enormous healing power.

WATER-CRYSTAL PHOTOGRAPHY

For many years now I've been studying the healing power of water. I was the first scientist in Japan to use a device that made it possible to transfer vibrations into this substance. Thanks to this water, which was charged with "healing" information, many people who came to see me in my practice were restored to health.

Water has played a central role in my life for a long time. I've often noticed that as long as we're receptive and open, we can often uncover very valuable clues in even the smallest things around us. This happened to me one day when I read: "No two snow crystals are the same." Of course, I'd learned that as a child in school. I knew that each snowflake was unique. But at that very moment, the sentence had a completely new meaning to me. Suddenly I realized that the snowflake state revealed the individual face of each water drop, and that it might be possible to take photographs of it. My hypothesis was that the ice crystals would give me information about the *state* of the water. This idea gripped me—I wanted to freeze water and then try to take pictures of the crystals. So I rented a high-resolution microscope and started some experiments with the assistance of a young researcher from my company.

Two long months went by with no results whatsoever, but one day my radiant co-worker presented me with the first photo of a water crystal. Looking back now, it seems a miracle that we even managed to get pictures, considering the conditions under which the experiment was first carried out!

We started by putting a single drop of water in each of the 50 petri dishes we'd prepared. We then froze them at a temperature of –13° F and took pictures under the microscope of the crystals that had formed. The temperature in the laboratory where we took the photographs was constantly kept at 23°F; even so, the average lifetime of a crystal under the microscope was just two minutes because of the light that was needed—this had a warming effect, which melted the subject.

In my other books, I've already explained that we normally chose just one out of some 50 pictures. Usually we decided on one that was representative of the shape that appeared most frequently.

THE MEMORY OF MEMORY

When water freezes, its molecules systematically connect and form the nucleons of a crystal; it becomes stable when it has the structure of a hexagon. Then it starts to grow and a visible crystal appears. This is the natural course of the procedure. However, if unnatural information is forced upon it, it's not able to form a harmonic hexagonal crystal.

Once our initial hypothesis had been confirmed by the data, I started to investigate water from different places. Our experiments went well and we managed to produce reliable pictures. The question we asked ourselves was: *Do water crystals look different under different circumstances?*

All my expectations were surpassed. The photographs clearly showed that depending on its origins (that is, whether it came from a natural spring or from the kitchen tap), water would take on a completely different shape. This was visible proof that not all water was the same—it reacted to the "experiences" it went through during its journey and stored that information. Water from a spring formed breathtakingly beautiful regular hexagons, while water from the lower course of a river or from a dam hardly achieved a complete crystal. The most shocking results came from chloride-ridden drinking water. It can be really painful to see water that has been mistreated in such a way if you know what marvelous crystals natural water can form. . . .

Above: This is how the crystal pictures are produced. The temperature is kept constant at -5° C in the laboratory. The photo must be taken very fast, because the beautiful crystal structure only lasts for two minutes.

This picture shows a water crystal, which was "given a soul" by labeling it with the word *thanks*. The result is this beautifully formed crystal.

This crystal was formed after the water has seen the picture with the jumping dolphins. The dolphin has a similar—or even higher—intelligence than the human being, and it's said that dolphins can heal us.

In light of these experiments, we can say that water has a memory. Each molecule of it carries some information, and when we drink it, that data becomes part of our body. Looking at these pictures, ask yourself: "Which information do I want to take in?"

WATER LISTENS TO MUSIC

One day, Dr. Ishibashi, the chemist and scientist who took the photographs of the water crystals, came to see me and asked, "What if we played some music to the water?" I found the idea terrific and that's how some of the most impressive pictures came into being (see the following photos).

Schubert's interpretation of "Ave Maria." This picture shows a very beautiful, symmetric crystal, which radiates deep love.

Water listens to *Swan Lake* by Tchaikovsky and a crystal is formed with delicate branches, reminiscent of swans' necks.

This water listened to the CD *Message from Water*. If you look into the center, you can see another small crystal trying to form itself.

Crystals responding to the *Four Seasons* music.

Above: Spring: The plants starting to sprout.

Right, top to bottom: Summer: They reach full blossom, Autumn: The seeds have developed and start to drop from the plant, Winter: The seeds rest hidden away in the winter. It's the time for retreat and silence.

The Beatles, "Yesterday": A beautiful crystal has formed. The structure of the turtle shell shows that this music strengthens the immune system.

"Edelweiss" from *The Sound of Music: Edelweiss* means "precious white." In correspondence with this name, a very clear white crystal has formed. The center seems like a mirror.

The method was fairly simple: A small bottle of distilled water was placed between two loudspeakers, and music was then played. We discovered that if we knocked gently on the bottle before and after playing the music, we got clearer pictures.

We chose classical music for our first attempts and later on used popular contemporary music. Our choices ranged from Gregorian chants and Buddhist sutras to heavy metal. We also experimented with healing melodies. We discovered, for example, that some pieces of music supported the immune system. Sound is vibration, so we now know that water is able to react to vibrations and can store them in its own very specific way. You can find out more about this in my other books.

When we started to act on the idea of playing music to water, we abandoned our role as passive observers for good.

IS WATER ABLE TO READ?

This question seemed absurd at first. However, I had the idea of showing some Japanese characters to water. In Japan, we think that every single word possesses a soul. I'll try to explain this by means

of an example. Let's take the word *gratitude.* When I say it, I haven't just given sound to a string of phonemes, but have expressed a meaning and a feeling. We believe that a word possesses this power of transmission because it has a share of the word soul and is its messenger or, more accurately, its representative. By saying "Thank you," I step into resonance with this word *soul* and vibrate in unison with it. And, as I'd expected, water shown a range of different Japanese characters formed completely different crystals.

THE WORD SOUL AND MORPHOGENETIC FIELDS

I'm always fascinated to see how ancient wisdom is being rediscovered by some brave scientists of our time. Biologist Rupert Sheldrake speaks about a morphogenetic field, in which all information is stored in the shape of vibrations. The morphogenetic field for "Thank you" is increased if somebody says the words—or just even thinks them. The stronger a morphogenetic field, the easier it becomes for everybody else to say those particular words and the more likely it is that this will happen.[1]

An example of this is the phenomenon of the hundredth monkey, as first observed in the late 1950s on a northern Japanese island. A group of behavioral scientists observed that monkeys on the island would wash their potatoes before they ate them. It's likely that one of them started it by chance, and then others copied its behavior. They must have found out that the taste of a washed potato was far better than one that hadn't been cleaned. Eventually, there were 100 monkeys on that island who were eating in this fashion. Then something fascinating happened: Suddenly, monkeys on another island started to wash their potatoes; but they didn't start one by one, as had been the case on the first island, but all at once, as if the animals on the first island had told them about their discovery. However, there had been no contact between the two groups.

This phenomenon can be used to explain the theory behind the morphogenetic field. Through the behavior of the first group of monkeys, a field of vibrations was created that contained the information "Washed potatoes taste good." At a certain critical mass (the hundredth monkey), the field developed an intensity that allowed others to have a share in this information.

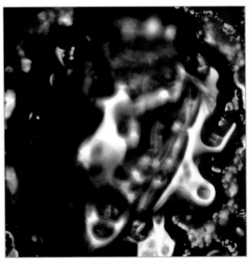

Above: This water was given a label with the word *demon.* Judge for yourself how this word affected the water.

Right, top to bottom: Om Namah Shivaya is a Sanskrit mantra. This beautiful crystal looks like a mandala. *Next:* This crystal was formed using a label with the words "This is really beautiful." One can wholeheartedly agree! *Last:* **Power:** Here you can see that power on its own can't achieve anything—no ordered crystal structure has formed.

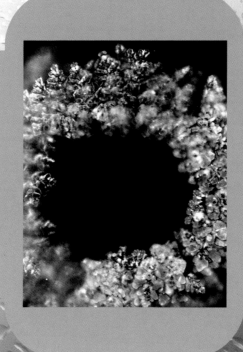

Soul: This crystal grew very fast and shows a spectacular play of colors.

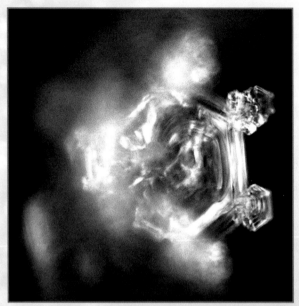

Water with the label "bad luck." A very weak crystal has formed, which is trying unsuccessfully to bring itself into balance.

Lucky: This is perfect beauty and harmony. Like a fine-cut diamond. Maybe harmony is a necessity for luck. . . .

In the same way that actions originate a morphogenetic field, so do words; and each word makes its own individual contribution. We can imagine this as similar to a hologram in which every single piece describes the whole picture.

A professor from Yale University wanted to test Rupert Sheldrake's theory. He put together a range of Hebrew words and a similar number of meaningless, invented words. He then mixed these two sets and showed them to some students, one word at a time. (None of the subjects could speak Hebrew.) He asked them to try to guess the meaning of each word and didn't tell them that some of them were totally meaningless.[2] With the Hebrew words, there was a statistical approximation of the correct meaning, while it was obvious (by means of the statistical distribution of the answers) that the students had used guesswork on the words without any meaning. This was a confirmation of Sheldrake's theory of the morphogenetic field, or what I described as the "word soul."

I believe it's this word *soul,* this vibrational information, that the water reads and tunes in to. The results of this tuning in are then visible in the different water crystals. Actually, we can see the pattern of vibration of the specific word soul, and it feels to me as if a window opens up and we can get a glimpse of the universe.

THE POWER OF THE WORD SOUL

When we're thinking a thought and give it energy by imagining it as real or speaking it, we're storing the pattern of vibration in the water of our bodies, and it shows as the corresponding vibration all around us and further out, beyond our physical selves. In this way, we influence our surroundings and others react to it, so we receive the appropriate feedback that again reinforces both our vibrations and the morphogenetic field. This shows how important it is to think and speak with purity of intent.

My esteemed teacher Dr. Nobuo Shioya made me aware of this a long time ago; and now, thanks to the water-crystal images, we can actually see it in solid form. In his book, *Der Jungbrunnen*

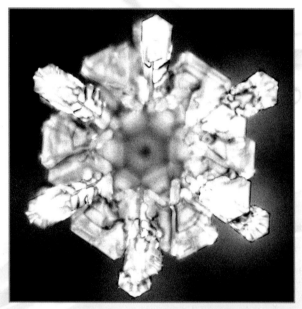

The healing hands of the mother: This powerful crystal shows a slight pink coloring. Pink is assigned to love and the energy of friendliness, which comes from the heart. It's also said that this color helps activate the life energy.

Giving birth: This picture shows that giving birth is more than simply delivering a baby. It feels as if a decision has been made to weave its own pattern of life. This picture shows a dynamic, developing movement.

des Dr. Shioya (*Dr. Shioya's Fountain of Youth*), Dr. Shioya describes the three "correct states of mind" that can help each of us live a happier life. Although very ill from birth, he developed a breathing technique that he combined with visualization. This method of "creative power thoughts and correct breathing" made it possible for him to live a healthier and longer life. From his 60th birthday onward, he really started to rejuvenate. For example, he won a golf tournament at the venerable age of 100 years.

DR. SHIOYA'S THREE GOLDEN RULES

Dr. Shioya's three correct states of mind are fundamental attitudes that are easy to adopt and can bring about an enormous change in our everyday life. Their meaning and use will become even more apparent in the light of our knowledge about the power of the word soul.

1. *Be positive.* It's proven that positive thoughts influence our physical health. For example, they can strengthen the immune system. This state of mind isn't an instruction to lead a "better" life (in a religious or moral sense), but a powerful aid to maintaining good health in both body and mind. By having a positive attitude and being open to all situations, we're prepared to recognize

Dr. Nobu Shioya: With the help of his simple method of "creative power of the thoughts and the right way of breathing," it's possible to rejuvenate the body and mind.

opportunities and take them. This has nothing to do with superficial politeness or trite "seeing life through rose-tinted glasses"—quite the opposite, actually. Instead of focusing just on the negative, we look at *both sides* of the proverbial coin. By doing so, we learn to recognize the possibilities available to us.

2. *Don't forget to say thank you.* Gratitude can be a core feeling, and it's important to always remind ourselves of it. Awareness generates energy. If we're consciously grateful, we send out corresponding vibrations and attract similar vibrations. This means that we'll find ourselves in more and more situations where we have a good reason to give thanks. Anyone who lacks this basic attitude should turn their attention to things they can be grateful for, however small they are. Some people might claim that there's absolutely nothing in their lives that falls into this category, but actually we can give thanks that we are alive every day.

3. *Don't nag.* If we find fault with everything instead of being grateful, these thoughts and feelings become vibrations that are sent out and in turn attract situations that will lead to more nagging. Thoughts such as *I'm in trouble, I don't like this, I can't do it, This is hard,* or *This is laborious* will attract difficult, unpleasant, hard, and laborious situations.

The water-crystal images show us the effect on water of, for example, the word *fool* or a phrase like "We have done this really well." The same vibration is created when we say to somebody, "You are a fool." This isn't just a statement per se; by uttering the words we create, or rather reinforce, the negative vibration, and thus the very pattern of behavior. These disharmonic patterns of vibration are "stamped" on water in general and on the bodily waters of the person in question.

This is the effect of the word *fool*. Water can't form a
crystal structure if words are hurtful and belittling.

The main reason why I always argue that we should praise
our children (and friends and colleagues) is because we thereby
reinforce their positive qualities. I'm certain that we'd all benefit
from this kind of consciousness in speech and thought, especially
as words and thoughts that are aimed at somebody else always
have an impact on us first. If I were to give out the word *fool* into
the world, my own system would be filled with this vibration first
and would come into step with its disharmonic content.

The time-honored principle "Do unto others as you would
have them do unto you" acquires a completely new meaning
in the light of the theory of the morphogenetic field. Even the
most self-centered person has the ability to speak, act, and think
considerately—and should do so, because it should be clear by now
that we are responsible for what happens to us.

Another mental habit that hinders self-development is the
practice of running ourselves down, both verbally and internally.
Every one of us has the ability (and perhaps I should also say the

duty to ourselves) to speak and act in such a way that nurtures, rather than poisons, our microcosm. I'm always saddened by the realization that so many people invest so much of their inner energy running themselves down both verbally and internally, just because something didn't happen in the way that they'd hoped. By doing this we don't create the flow of positive energy that can help us learn from our mistakes. If we look at water crystals, the message is clear: We poison ourselves with all this negative chatter.

The time is now ripe to put this realization into practice and break the habit of a lifetime. It's not my intention to preach here: Water itself speaks a distinct and clear language. Life isn't really that complicated, and we all carry that knowledge inside ourselves; we just have to rediscover it. The pictures of the water crystals can help us in the search for our own truth. They can guide us.

THE NEW HEALING POWER: THE DIALOGUE WITH WATER

The healing power of water and its ability to carry information has been known for centuries, and many therapies have been based on this knowledge. What's new is that these "hidden" properties can now be made visible. The information carried by the water can be seen as a picture, and this changes our view of it from a mere chemical molecule into a living creature.

In former times there was nothing unusual in holding conversations with nature and nature spirits, even in the Western world. Nowadays, our increasingly mechanistic view of things prevents us from acknowledging these organic perceptions, even if they come into our consciousness. Nothing can be what it's not allowed to be.

The water-crystal images act as mediators between those of us who are still caught in this mechanistic view of the world and the holographic reality. By "holographic" I mean that you can see the whole of the picture in every part. The images of the water crystals are ambassadors, giving us an insight into the real connections of the universe.

People want to feel safe—that's why a clear philosophy of the life of the world was developed. A new age has now come into being. We can no longer close ourselves to a broader philosophy of life, and we can now find that longed-for safety at a higher level. If we learn how to tune in to this elevated vibration, we can become one with it.

Water is a very honest mirror. The pictures of the water crystals show clearly the effects that different environmental factors have on living systems. But what these images show as well is that we're not helplessly exposed to these negative influences. Through love and gratitude, we have the ability to improve our world. By thinking and feeling "love and gratitude," we can actively put a healing process into motion.

When we look at the water-crystal pictures of negative ideas, the numinous fear that most of us feel disappears. Instead, we empathize with the malformed water. It didn't choose to suffer in such a manner. In this way, a new state of mind comes into being inside us. We want to do something good for the water and, consequently, for ourselves. We're not at war anymore with the pollution of negativity. Conflict just produces more harmful energy, which in turn gives rise to more adversity. We don't want to close our eyes to the negative—on the contrary, we're visually and intellectually aware of it—but we use love and gratitude to transform it in a positive way.

From this it follows that we have the ability to take an active part in the creation of our world. This realization gives us not only power but also responsibility. We are no longer helpless "playthings." What kind of existence do we want to create? What do we want to put into being? *Each* of us is called on to answer this basic question in thought, word, and deed. If I yearn for peace but nag and scold and condemn all the time, then how can my dream come into being, either in myself or anywhere else?

The pictures of the water crystals stimulate our imagination. We're so controlled by the left side of our brain, but images affect the right side, and many have the effect of mandalas. I would have preferred to show only beautiful photos, but I thought it was also important to give the left part of the brain some good stuff to ponder, and therefore to question old thinking patterns. In this way the pictures of the water crystals have an effect on our whole mental structure. Simply reading something is one-sided, as is just looking at pictures. It's only from the combination of both that new realizations can grow and be put into practice in our everyday lives. These images carry a message that reaches us at the mental, soul, and physical levels through the water in our bodies that vibrates in harmony with them.

Like children going through the "Why?" phase of development, we, too, can ask water everything that's important to us. In this way we can gain an insight into reality as it truly is. Water is a messenger—it brings us information about the world and the universe.

LIFE IS MOVEMENT

Ancient wisdom shows itself clearly in the crystals. Water from a free-flowing river creates incredibly beautiful shapes. If we examine the formations from the stagnating area of a dam, we don't find any crystal structures—the pictures here are similar to looking through a hole dug in a swamp. By not being allowed to flow, water loses its vitality, its charisma. It's cut off from the river of life. And the same applies to us as human beings: It's vital for us, too, to move with the universal current. Each stagnation brings a dying off.

We know this at a physical level. For example, when the blood becomes too thick and clots form in our arteries and veins, the risk of a heart attack or stroke increases. We know this at an emotional level, too. If a person is holding on to a feeling—say, grief—he or she will one day stiffen with the pain. The same happens mentally, as there are those who become rigid with fear, dogma, and prejudice. The water crystals show us very clearly how we should live—what's good for the water in nature is also good for that element in our bodies. Being in constant motion at all levels contributes significantly to our well-being.

By doing this, we're not only helping ourselves, but also water in general. By giving the water in our bodies the necessary attention, we honor the water of Earth, too, because everything is connected. We're aquatic beings, and I can't stress enough the importance of becoming aware of it. The consequence should be that we treat the gift of the universe respectfully and attentively and honor its wisdom.

OFFERING LOVE AND GRATITUDE TO WATER

I firmly believe that it's our duty as human beings to contribute to the healing of the earth and its waters. For many of us this has been a need for a long time. Now we know that together we can make big things happen, as the law of the hundredth monkey teaches us.

One of the most important messages that we receive from the water crystals is that each of our thoughts, words, and actions represents information that we send out. Our consciousness has a real influence on water, which becomes particularly powerful when many of us become one and aim for the same goal. In this lies the power of joint prayer. Let's use this energy to give love and gratitude to water.

Let's declare July 25 of each year a "World Day of Love and Thanks to Water." We'll start this event with a ceremony to send out our feelings to the life-giving liquid and in this way gradually raise our consciousness. Take part in it on your own or with others, and direct your thoughts and prayers to water. Every single person counts; each loving word matters. All drops that are treated with love and respect carry those vibrations out into the world.

To increase the power of the message, I suggest sending out the vibrations three times during the day, say at 7 A.M., 1 P.M., and 7 P.M. (your local time). Please direct love and thanks to water at one or all of these times and pass this information on to all those who are interested.

How you arrange the ceremony is completely up to you. You can say prayers from your own religion, or you can do a visualization. I, for instance, imagine silver/golden light filling water and the earth and flowing out of the heart of each and every person.

In addition to this World Day of Love and Thanks to Water, let's send out our affection and gratitude at the same times on the 25th of each month. By doing so, you're also benefitting yourself: You're lifting your own vibration. And by thanking the water that, for example, runs over your hands while you're washing up, you're appreciating the same substance in your body, in your cells. In that way you're contributing actively to your own well-being.

The health of each and every person is one of my most heartfelt wishes. But an even more important desire is for healing the natural world, Earth, and humanity as a whole. My dream is one of world peace, and I know that I'm not alone in this.

○ ○ ○

NOTES

1. The morphogenetic field, or morphic resonance, is a name given to a form of action at a distance proposed by Rupert Sheldrake. However, the idea that vision is a two-way process has been held by a great many minds in the past. The theory states that things of the same "form" tend to "resonate" with each other, so that, for example:

> When crystals of a newly synthesized chemical substance, for example a new kind of drug, arise for the first time they have no exact precedent, but as the same compound is crystallized again and again, the crystals should tend to form more readily all over the world, just because they have already formed somewhere else. (Rupert Sheldrake, *The Presence of the Past*, HarperCollins, 1988)

This concept defies, among other things, the theory of special relativity—all crystals, all over the universe, regardless of distance in space/time, will be affected.

The theory of the morphogenetic field, first conceptualized by developmental biologists (beginning in the mid-1980s), seems to be accumulating evidence that it's closely linked to the quantum gravitational field:

A. The field pervades all space.

B. The field interacts with all matter and energy, irrespective of whether or not that matter/energy is magnetically charged.

C. And, most significantly, the field is what's known mathematically as a "symmetric second-rank tensor."

All three properties are characteristic of gravity, and it was proven some years ago that the only self-consistent nonlinear theory of a symmetric second-rank tensor field is, at least at low energies, precisely Einstein's general relativity. Thus, if the evidence for A, B, and C becomes validated, we can infer that the morphogenetic field is the quantum counterpart of Einstein's gravitational field.

2. See the Website **www.co-intelligence.org/P-more onmorphgnicflds.html** for more information on Gary Schwartz's experiment with Hebrew words.

PART I

SCIENTIFIC PERSPECTIVES

INTRODUCTION

Anyone who can remember their science lessons—whether in chemistry, physics, or biology—may recall that water was largely ignored or taken for granted as an inert, simple substance with the formula H_2O. Of course it had a few other properties, such as a boiling point of 100°C, and a unique way of expanding and contracting as it froze and unfroze. We knew it as central, not only to all life on Earth, but also to the planet's many geological processes. The unspoken message was: *That's just the way things are—no need to ask why!*

In recent years, a few brave scientists, risking ridicule and ruin, have been pioneers in discovering a whole new world with respect to the properties of water. Among the first of these was the French immunologist Jacques Benveniste, who attempted to prove that water had memory and could retain information about complex chemicals, even if there was no trace left of them. This was seen as scientific heresy, and for his trouble, Benveniste was dismissed from his job, and his laboratory was closed down. He died in 2004, but his conclusions proved so intriguing that many claim to have successfully repeated his experiments.

Other scientists followed in his footsteps, and some of the most distinguished of these have contributed to this book. In most cases, the authors have done much to simplify technical papers so that lay readers can follow them, and it's well worth a little extra time and effort to digest the contents. Having done so, you, the reader, will see something amazing—the beginnings of a whole new understanding of the world and life on it, going far beyond the limitations of the current materialist scientific era. In this new vision, thought and consciousness profoundly affect not only the structure of water, but also many other substances, even playing a critical role in the way DNA decodes itself in new life. We stand at the dawn of a new era, one that will profoundly change not only science, but also our spirituality, and indeed our whole culture.

I'm profoundly honored that my own books have been able to reach out to a wider readership around the world, demonstrating the power of thought, prayer, and intention to change water for the benefit of us all.

— Masaru Emoto

CHAPTER 1

PSYCHOENERGETIC SCIENCE: EXPANDING TODAY'S SCIENCE TO INCLUDE HUMAN CONSCIOUSNESS

by William A. Tiller, Ph.D.

Psychoenergetic science is an expansion of today's conventional science, which for 400 years has dealt with the following metaphorical reaction equation:

$$\textbf{MASS} \rightleftarrows \textbf{ENERGY} \qquad\qquad (1a)$$

Psychoenergetic science deals with this expanded reaction equation:

$$\textbf{MASS} \rightleftarrows \textbf{ENERGY} \rightleftarrows \textbf{CONSCIOUSNESS} \qquad (1b)$$

Experience shows that human consciousness readily manipulates **information** of all kinds (numbers to sums, language letters to make words and sentences, jigsaw-puzzle pieces to make maps and pictures, and symbols to make equations) to produce order out of disorder[1-5]. From our psychoenergetics research, which is outlined in the first part of this article, we have discovered a second, unique level of physical reality that is quite different from our normal electric atom/molecule level. This new level functions in the physical vacuum within the "empty" space between the fundamental particles that make up atoms and molecules. The stuff of this physical vacuum consists of magnetic information waves; and we've observed that the physics of this new level is modulatable by the human mind, intentions, and consciousness in general.

About eight years ago, we discovered a reliable, repeatable procedure for lifting the electromagnetic symmetry state of a room or other large space higher than that of our normal atom/molecule level to one wherein commercial instrument measurements became capable of accessing these two unique levels of physical reality. In addition, this procedure allowed us to tune this large space so that a specific intention could be manifested in that place via the physics of this vacuum level of physical reality. From our research, we have found that a specific material property consists of two parts: one from the electric atom/molecule level of physical reality (which is all our normal world can presently measure), and one from the magnetic information wave level of physical reality. The instrumentally accessed magnitude of this second contribution depends on the magnitude of a special coupling coefficient material connecting these two levels. This coupling coefficient can be of negligible magnitude, as in our normal level of physical reality, or, via utilizing the aforementioned intention procedure, can be caused to be of large magnitude. We have utilized this new procedure to:

1. Substantially change the pH of the same type of water in equilibrium with air either up or down by one full pH unit (~100 times our measurement accuracy)

2. Increase by ~25% ($p < 0.001$) the in vitro thermodynamic activity of a specific human liver enzyme, alkaline phosphatase

3. Increase by ~20% ($p < 0.001$) the in vivo [ATP]/[ADP] ratio in the cells of fruit-fly larvae so that they would be fitter and have a much shorter (~20% at $p < 0.001$) development time to the adult fly stage; here, ATP is the energy storage molecule in all cells while ADP is its chemical precursor

In addition to the foregoing, we've discovered that humans, and perhaps all vertebrates, have their acupuncture meridian/chakra system at this higher electromagnetic symmetry state, so humans have the basic capability to do what our intention-device does—though perhaps not to such a significant degree unless they're at a master or avatar level of self-development. We hoped to be able to convert our detection device into a stand-alone engineered system for use as an individual or group biofeedback device to enhance individual (or group) self-development to higher and higher levels of inner self-management.

Finally, in the second part of this article, I provide a brief theoretical overview of what controls ice-crystal shape during the freezing of water, both without and with the application of human intention.

PART I: KEY BACKGROUND EXPERIMENTAL DATA

References 7 to 9 cover my psychoenergetics research books over the past 35 years. In the first contribution,[7] the work clearly showed that human consciousness could enhance the radiation spectra of the human biofield sufficiently to have a robust impact on a wide variety of physical processes. Table 1 provides a summary of these key experimental findings. The second contribution[8] covers the period from 1997 to 2001, and Table 2 provides a summary of our key experimental findings during that period.

TABLE 1: SUMMARY OF KEY EXPERIMENTAL FINDINGS FROM "SCIENCE AND HUMAN TRANSFORMATION"

1. A highly developed human biofield can alter the properties of materials and the functioning of devices so as to reveal deeper levels of nature not anticipated from our normal, everyday observations. The radiations from such levels of nature pass through materials that are optically opaque to EM radiations in the visible range.

2. Non-EM emissions from the biofields of normal humans, when modulated by their attention and directed intention, can enhance or not enhance electron microavalanches in a simple gas discharge device, depending upon the actual focus of the humans' intention.

3. Some humans emit bursts of subtle energy from various body chakras; and via a subtle energy/electrical energy conversion process involving the acupuncture meridian system, large voltage pulses appear both on the body and at sites remote from the body.

4. When focusing on the heart with loving intent, the human EKG becomes harmonic at the baroreflex frequency, 0.14 hertz, where the heart entrains the brain, and simultaneously all the other major electrophysiological systems of the body. In this heart-entrainment mode of functioning, body-chemical production becomes healthier, and focused intent can psychokinetically influence molecular structures both inside and outside the body.

5. Most young children perceive both EM and subtle energies. Lens and prism experiments indicate that the latter travel at velocities, $v>c$, the EM light velocity, and speed up on entering denser matter.

6. Dowsing is a natural human body response mechanism for those who give it meaning, wherein the unconscious communicates valuable information to the conscious via involuntary small muscle movements or the creation of localized heat patterns.

TABLE 2: SUMMARY OF KEY EXPERIMENTAL FINDINGS FROM "CONSCIOUS ACTS OF CREATION"

1. Human consciousness, in the form of a specific intention, can be imprinted into a simple, low-tech electronic device from a deep meditative state by highly inner self-managed humans. Such a device, now called an IIED (intention imprinted electrical device), can act as an effective surrogate to robustly influence a unique target experiment in physical reality.

2. The four unique target experiments studied involved (a) an inorganic material (water) with property changes 100 times larger than measurement accuracy, (b) an organic in vitro material with property changes of ~20% at p<0.001, and (c) a living in vivo material with property changes of ~20% at p<0.001, both of the latter having a built-in control.

3. A unique intelligence was present in an IIED after imprinting so that the measured material property changes were (a) always in the direction of the IIED's intention imprint and (b) always specific to the particular IIED utilized.

4. An unshielded IIED in the electrically "off" state, and physically separated from a UED (unimprinted electrical device) in the electrically "off" state by ~100 meters, still has a communication channel available to it for transferring the imprint statement to the UED within a week. Thus, the carrier for such information exchange is not conventional electromagnetism.

5. This new field, although not EM, can be dissipated through EM-leakage pathways. Thus, wrapping an IIED in aluminum foil and storing it in an electrically

grounded Faraday cage prolongs its lifetime of effective use (~3 months before reimprinting is required).

6. Placing a specific IIED in a room and turning it on "conditions" the room to a state wherein Item 2 in this table naturally manifests. Without the presence of this "conditioned" state in the room housing the target experiment equipment, these material property changes don't occur.

7. One characteristic of a "conditioned" space is that a DC magnetic field polarity effect on the pH of water occurs. Such an effect is thought to require the accessing of magnetic monopoles, a property usually associated with a higher EM gauge symmetry state than our normal, everyday reality. Such a higher EM gauge symmetry state is also a higher thermodynamic free energy per unit volume state.

8. Another characteristic of a "conditioned" space is the spontaneous appearance of material property oscillations of very large amplitude (air and water temperature, pH, electrical conductivity of water, etc.) that are (a) global throughout the room, (b) all exhibit the same Fourier spectral components, and (c) all are in the frequency range ~10^{-2} to 10^{-3} hertz.

9. A third important characteristic of a "conditioned" space is that it's sensitive to the presence of an active IIED at separation distances of at least ~150 feet. Oscillations generated in the locale of the IIED spontaneously appear (at high correlation coefficient) in a "conditioned" space but not in an unconditioned space.

10. If the degree of "conditioning" in a space is low and the IIED is removed from the space, the "conditioning"

decays slowly with a time constant of ~1 month. If the degree of "conditioning" in a space is sufficiently high, the IIED can be completely removed from the space and stored properly and the level of "conditioning" in the room doesn't appear to change (at least for 1–2 years).

11. The cause of the air temperature oscillations in a "conditioned" space near an apparent source was shown not to depend upon movements of the air molecules in the space, but rather thought to depend on changes at the vacuum level of physical reality.

12. Removal of the apparent air temperature oscillation source revealed that this vacuum level "phantom" source had a very slow relaxation time (~1–2 months) back to zero amplitude.

13. While in the phantom temperature oscillation source mode of reality, abrupt changes in the orientation of a large natural quartz crystal placed in the initial source region showed abrupt changes in overall oscillation wave shape, amplitude, and frequency. Thus, a quartz crystal appears to be a type of "tuner" for this vacuum-source behavior.

14. In a "conditioned" space, spontaneous and abrupt shifts in computer monitoring behavior of a random number generator (RNG) occurred from time to time for no apparent reason.

15. Experimenter effect, specific materials effects, and specific device effects appeared, in the short term, to alter the "tuning" of the oscillations in a conditioned space.

This particular body of work showed that human consciousness, in the form of a specific and detailed intention, could be imprinted into a very simple electronic device from a deep meditative state and then this processed device (now called an IIED, intention imprinted electrical device) could act as a surrogate for the specific intention and thereafter robustly influence a specifically designed target experiment in full accord with the intention imprinted therein. Figure 1 illustrates the general behavior for four distinctly different target experiments.

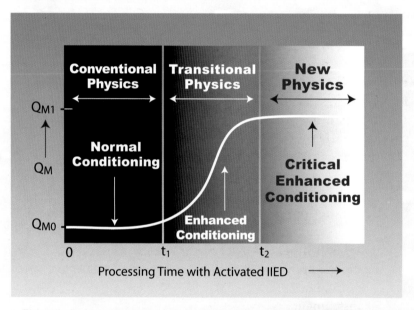

Figure 1: Q_M (some generalized physical measurement) vs. IIED processing time (length of time a space experiences a process leading to enhanced coupling)

Surprisingly, it was found that placing this IIED ~100 meters from a physically identical but unimprinted device, with both in the electrically switched-off state, didn't inhibit transfer of the specific intention imprint from the IIED to the unimprinted device within less than a week. This implies that a new information channel, other than conventional Maxwellian electromagnetism (EM), is present in nature for such an information change to occur. This new information carrier appears to be one that's modulatable by human intent. The basic process of electrically turning on an

IIED in a given laboratory space causes this space to be "IIED-conditioned" in such a way as to allow the instrumentation present in that space to access another level of physical reality after an ~3 month period of such space conditioning. The particular material property targeted by the specific intention imbedded in the device varies over time according to Figure 1 and the following equation:

$$Q_M = Q_{P1} + \propto_{eff} Q_{P2} \tag{2}$$

In Equation 2, Q_M is the total instrumentally measured value of the property, Q_{P1} is the normal value, Q_{M0}, in Figure 1, Q_{P2} is the expectation value for this second level of physical reality while $\propto_{eff}$ is the coupling coefficient between these two unique levels of physical reality. Relative to Figure 1, $\propto_{eff} Q_{P2}$ is $(Q_{M1} - Q_{M0})$, the intention magnitude of property change imprinted into the particular IIED. A fully IIED-conditioned laboratory has been observed to exhibit several characteristic signatures:

1. $Q_{P2}(t)$ is responsive to the polarity of a DC magnetic field placed close to the pH-measuring instruments; i.e., Q_{P2} (north-pole up) – Q_{P2} (south pole up) $\neq 0$ as it should for our normal reality (Q_{P1}) because there only magnetic dipoles are present. To yield such an experimental result, magnetic monopoles must also be present and instrumentally accessible.

2. Temporal material property oscillations of very large magnitude appear for pH(t), $\sigma(t)$, $T_W(t)$, and $T_A(t)$, (where σ = electrical conductivity, T_W is water temperature and T_A is air temperature) are (a) global throughout the room, (b) all exhibit the same Fourier spectral components, and (c) all components are in the frequency range ~10^{-2} to 10^{-3} hertz.

3. The $T_A(t)$ oscillations (magnitude ~3°C) were shown, via a forced convection experiment, not to be due to any natural convection process in the room's air and

remained for weeks to months after the supposed source of the oscillations had been removed from the experimental space.

4. For these phantom $T_A(t)$ oscillations, it was observed that when a large natural quartz crystal was placed with its c-axis pointing upwards in the initial "source" location, it just increased the $T_A(t)$ amplitude slightly and sharpened the spatial $T_A(t)$ profile somewhat. However, when the crystal was rotated 90° so that its c-axis was in the horizontal plane and aligned with the row of thermistors, there was an immediate inversion of the wave shape with reduction of the wave amplitude by a factor of ~2–3 and an increase of the wave frequency by a factor of ~3–5.

From these four main experimental observations, it was deduced that such phenomena weren't associated with the electric atom/molecule level of physical reality, but rather the coarse physical vacuum level of reality; i.e., from within the space unoccupied by the nucleons making up the atoms and molecules. Further, it was deduced that magnetic monopoles were intimately involved with the material nature of this coarse physical vacuum level of reality.

Reference 9 was our third major psychoenergetics contribution, and its contents cover the period ~2001 through 2004. Table 3 provides a summary of the key experimental findings collected in reference 9. This work largely focused on replication by others of the $\Delta pH = +1$ units experiments at several laboratories in the U.S. and Europe. Initially, three laboratories (Payson, Missouri, and Kansas) with such IIEDs were utilized; and each had a control site, containing identical pH-measurement equipment plus a UED (no IIED), located within ~2 to 20 miles of the IIED site. This experimental replication of the original Minnesota results[3] was successfully achieved. At these three sites $\Delta pH(t)$ grew exponentially with time to levels significantly above the normal theoretical value. However, at their control sites, the same type of behavior occurred, indicating that a macroscopic, room temperature information entanglement process occurred between the IIED sites and their UED sites.

Next, the Baltimore and Bethesda sites were initially used as control sites for the three IIED sites; and within ~2 months, the same large increase in ΔpH with exponential time-dependence for pH(t) occurred at these sites. Finally, the U.K. and Milan site (three months later) were initially used as control sites for the system; and within three weeks for the U.K. site and one week for the Milan site, pH(t) was exponentially increasing with time and ΔpH reached ~1 pH units. Now the information entanglement process between sites had been proven to reach ~6,000 miles.

TABLE 3: SUMMARY OF KEY EXPERIMENTAL FINDINGS FROM SOME SCIENCE ADVENTURES WITH REAL MAGIC

1. The original Minnesota water pH results have been substantially replicated by others.

2. At all remote IIED sites, the digitally recorded pH for purified water in equilibrium with air increased exponentially with time, with the ΔpH increasing cycle by cycle of water change until it reached ~1.0 pH units.

3. At all control sites (non-IIED sites), the same type of pH-behavior was observed via an information entanglement process except that (1) for below-ground sites, ΔpH achieved ~1.7 pH units and (2) for well-above-ground sites, ΔpH achieved only ~0.8 pH units.

4. This information entanglement process between IIED and non-IIED control sites of the overall experimental system occurred over distances from ~2 miles to ~6,000 miles. The carrier wave for this information transfer couldn't have been electromagnetic.

5. A litmus paper pH-detector only responded to the purely chemical level of the H+ content present in the water, while digital pH-detectors responded to both this level plus an information level associated with the H+ content.

6. All sites, both IIED and non-IIED, exhibited substantial values of $\Delta\Psi'_H+ = \Psi'_H - \eta_H+$ after a short time, indicating a raised thermodynamic-free energy per unit volume for all sites.

7. The time required to reach ΔpH ~1.0 pH units appears to be less for below-ground control sites than for above-ground control sites and also appears to be relatively independent of distance.

8. Strong experimenter and equipment potentization effects were noted.

9. The optimum reimprinting time for an IIED presently appears to be ~3 months.

10. Mu-metal screening does not shield water from this new information entanglement field.

11. For humans, and perhaps all vertebrates, bioelectro-magnetism is quite different from Maxwellian electro-magnetism, because the human acupuncture meridian system is observed to be at an EM gauge symmetry level where magnetic monopole charge is experimentally accessible.

12. A laboratory space and equipment raised to an EM gauge symmetry state wherein magnetic monopole currents are experimentally accessible is found to be a very sensitive detector of subtle energy emissions by humans (subtle

energies are defined as all those beyond the energy aspects of the accepted four fundamental forces).

13. Large bursts of subtle energy emissions during healing steps in humans located in a "conditioned" laboratory act analogously to earthquakes with reverberating aftershocks that last for a long time. Thus, the detailed character of the laboratory's energy signature is significantly altered for a long time (greater than three months).

For those remote sites at ground level, the experimental data yielded $\Delta pH\infty$ = +1 pH unit; for those remote sites located three stories above ground level, only ΔpH = +0.8 pH units occurred; and for those remote sites below ground level (in a basement), ΔpH = +1.7 pH units occurred. Whatever this new type of energy is, it prefers to travel through the ground rather than through the air, in opposition to EM energy, which prefers to travel through the air.

During this replication experiment, we discovered both a theoretical and an experimental procedure for measuring $Q_{p2}(t)$ in Equation 2 for the hydrated proton and labeled it the magnetic monopole contribution to the magnetoelectrochemical potential energy for the hydrated proton $\Delta\Psi'_{H}+$.[4] Continuous values for this magnetic monopole contribution were determined for all sites, IIED and control, in the overall experimental system with initial magnitudes in the $\sim\pm5$ meV to ±40 meV range. By mid-2005, some of these values had grown to the ~80 meV range.

Finally, to close out this section, simple physical chemistry instruments located in an IIED-conditioned laboratory appear to be very sensitive detectors of biofield emissions from humans; and via kinesiological testing, various muscle groups were all shown to exhibit DC magnetic field polarity effects. This indicates that in all humans, and probably in all vertebrates, the acupuncture meridian/chakra system is at a significantly higher EM gauge symmetry level than the rest of the body. This means that human bioelectromagnetism is different from Maxwellian EM. This also means that the human mind can modulate this higher EM gauge state carrier wave, which is probably what is presently called Qi

(Chi), and this in turn can thermodynamically drive all varieties of processes at the electric atom/molecule level of the physical body.

THEORETICAL MODELING

The current formal description of quantum mechanics (QM) is completely inadequate to account for any psychoenergetic phenomenon.[9] However, if one assumes the simultaneous existence of particle and wave properties for physical matter, all QM phenomena can be quantitatively calculated and yield good agreement with experiment. Simultaneous QM and relativistic behavior calculations for the de Broglie particle/pilot wave concept yield the following[10]:

$$v_p v_w = c^2 \tag{3}$$

Here, v_p = the particle velocity, v_w is the velocity of the wave components making up the total pilot wave, and c is the velocity of electromagnetic (EM) light. Since relativity theory requires that $v_p < c$, always, Equation 3 requires that $v_w > c$ always. In order to avoid complications with relativity theory, these superluminal velocity wave components were dubbed "information waves" because it was thought that such waves could not transport energy. However, Equation 1b and the surrounding discussion indicate that this isn't correct. Adding item 7 of Table 2, we've labeled these waves as "magnetic information waves," which leads to the conundrum of how slower-than-light electric particles can interact with faster-than-light magnetic information waves to create the particle/pilot wave entity, a major cornerstone of QM. My resolution to this conundrum has been to postulate the existence of a substance called deltrons, from a domain beyond spacetime, that can travel both more slowly and more quickly than c. The slower-than-c portion of the deltron spectrum can interact with the electric particles while the faster-than-c portion of the deltron spectrum can interact with the magnetic information waves. This situation is illustrated in Figure 2, where one sees that meaningful interaction can occur across the light barrier via deltron-deltron interactions.

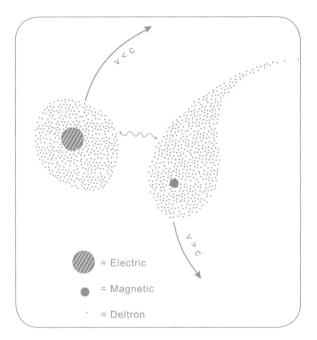

Figure 2: Illustration of deltron sheaths around both v < c and v > c moieties. Deltron-deltron interaction produces the coupling between such moieties.

Thus, the simplest component in physical reality is the electric particle/deltron/magnetic information wave complex. This is proposed to be the basic building block for all physical substances. The proposed new RF for meaningfully viewing such substances is (1) a duplex RF consisting of two reciprocal four-dimensional subspaces (one of which is spacetime) that is (2) embedded in the three higher dimensional domains of emotion (9D), mind (10D), and spirit (11D and above). Two illustrative representations of this new multidimensional RF are presented in Figures 3 and 4. The deltrons of the revisited de Broglie particle/pilot wave concept are proposed to be a natural moiety of the emotion domain, and they also constitute the coupler substance between the two levels P_1 and P_2 of physical reality.

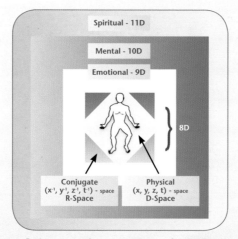

Figure 3: A structural representation of our RF with the duplex space in the center. Counting the duplex space as a unique member of the general 8-space, our RF is eleven-dimensional.

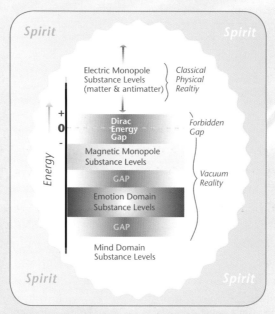

Figure 4: An energy-level diagram embracing both classical physical substances and "unseen" vacuum substances.

Using this proposed multidimensional RF, Figure 5 is the proposed mechanism for explaining how an IIED both (1) conditions a space so that $\propto_{eff}$, in Equation 1, is of a significant magnitude and

(2) tunes the space so that a specific material property of Level P_2 changes in magnitude to conform to the specific intention.

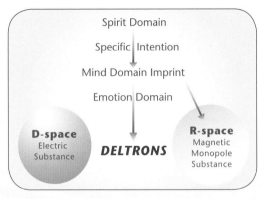

Figure 5: An intention imprint from the domain of spirit imprints a pattern on the domain of mind which, in turn, via a diffraction process, is thought to both activate deltrons and imprint a conjugate pattern on reciprocal space. The deltron enhancement couples this intent pattern to drive the atom/molecule processes in this level of physical reality.[2]

Here, the specific intention is generated at the level of spirit and is imprinted as a specific pattern on the domain of mind which, in turn, via a diffraction process, is proposed to both activate deltrons and imprint a conjugate pattern on reciprocal space. The deltron activation couples this intent pattern to drive the electric atom/molecule processes at the P_1 level of physical reality. This has been a very, very brief overview of our recent psychoenergetic science perspective; an order of magnitude of additional material on this subject can be found by perusing references 7 through 9.

PART II: SOME CONVENTIONAL SCIENCE, WITH REGARD TO CRYSTALLIZATION FROM AQUEOUS SOLUTIONS

To illustrate what fields of science and what general knowledge must be brought to bear for a reliable analysis of a crystal growth problem, a brief overview will be given here to indicate what controls a crystal's shape during unconstrained crystallization of water. For a more expanded view, the reader should explore references 11 to 13. For this "overview," we will be satisfied with a phenomenological description of the most important simultaneous processes involved in terms of "lumped" material parameters. Table 4 indicates the different areas of study necessary to be considered with the minimum number of involved materials parameters, macroscopic variables, and system constraints.

TABLE 4: CRYSTALLIZATION VARIABLES AND PARAMETERS

Area of Study	Boundary-value problems	Material parameters	Interface variables	Macroscopic variables	Constraints
Phase equilibria		$\Delta H, T_0, k_0, m_L$		$TL\,(C_\infty)$	
Nucleation		$N_0, \Delta T_C$		t	
Solute partitioning	Diffusion equation (C)	D_S, D_L, k_i	$C_i, T_L(C_i), V, S$	C_∞	
Fluid motion	Hydrodynamic equation (u)	v	δ_C	u_∞	C_∞
Excess solid free energy		$\gamma, \Delta S, \Sigma_i\,\gamma_i^f, \Sigma_i\,N_i^f$	T_E		$\dot{T}$
Interface attachment kinetics		μ_1, μ_2	T_i		
Heat transport	Heat equation (T)	$K_S, K_L, \alpha_X, \alpha_L$		T_∞	
Interface morphology	Perturbation response & coupling equations				
Defect generation	Stress equation				

ΔH is the latent heat of fusion, T_0 is the melting temperature of solvent, k_0 is the solute distribution coefficient, m_L is the liquidus slope, N_0 is a parameter related to area of nucleation catalyst surface, ΔT_C is a parameter related to potency of nucleation catalyst, k_i is the interface partition coefficient, D is the solute diffusivity, v is the kinematic viscosity, γ is the solid-to-liquid interfacial energy, ΔS is the entropy of fusion, γ_i^f is the fault energy, N_i^f is the number of faults of type I, μ is a parameter related to interface attachment kinetics, K is the thermal conductivity, and α is the heat diffusivity.

The conventional macroscopic variables that one either sets or controls are (1) the water chemical composition, C_∞, (2) the water cooling rate, $\dot{T}$, and (3) the shape of the container holding the fluid. Let us proceed with the process description by stages.

1. As the liquid is being cooled, we need to know the magnitude of the thermodynamic driving force for solid formation ΔG at any bath temperature T. This can be expressed as

$$\Delta G = f_1 [\Delta H, T_L (C_\infty)] \qquad (4a)$$

   where f_1 refers to the appropriate mathematical functional relationship between the latent heat of fusion, ΔH, and the liquidus temperature $T_L(C_\infty)$. Thus we see that phase equilibria data is one prerequisite. The material parameters needed for this area of study are listed and defined in Table 4.

2. As the bath undercooling, ΔT, increases with time, t, we need to know the undercooling at which particles of solid begin to form and also their density. Thus we must evaluate the nucleation frequency I, which can be most simply expressed as

$$I = f_2 (N_0, \Delta T_C, \dot{T}, t, C_\infty) \qquad (4b)$$

   where f_2 represents the appropriate functional relationship, N_0 is the number of atoms in contact with the foreign substrates that catalyzes the nucleation event, and ΔT_C is a parameter that defines the potency of the catalyst (the undercooling at which solid formation is initiated).

3. When the crystal illustrated in Figure 6 begins to grow at some velocity V, solute partitioning will occur at the interface since the equilibrium concentration of solute

in the solid C_S is different from the concentration in the liquid at the interface.

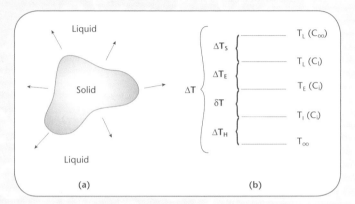

Left: Illustration of a crystal growing from a super-cooled liquid. *Right:* The important temperatures in a growth process. The magnitudes of the temperature differences indicate the degree of solute diffusion, capillarity, kinetic, or heat transport control.

Thus the concentration of solute in the liquid at the interface C_i must be determined and can be represented by a functional relationship of the form

$$\frac{C_i}{C_\infty} = f_3 \left(v,\ k_i,\ D, \delta_C,\ S^*, t \right) \tag{4c}$$

where k_i refers to an interface solute partition coefficient that is generally different from k_0 the phase diagram value, D is the solute diffusion coefficient, δ_C refers to the solute boundary layer thickness at the crystal surface, and S^* refers to the shape of the crystal.

4. In order to evaluate δ_C in Equation 4c, it is necessary to consider the hydrodynamics of the fluid. The fluid will generally exist in some state of motion, whether the driving force is applied by external means or arises naturally due to density variations in the fluid. We can consider the fluid far from the crystal-liquid interface to be moving with some relative stream velocity u_∞ due to

the average fluid body forces. The fluid motion will aid in the matter transport of solute away from the crystal into the bulk liquid and cause a lowering of C_i. We find that δ_C can be expressed as

$$\delta_C = f_4 \; (V, \, v, \, D, \, S^*, \, u_\infty, \, t) \tag{4d}$$

where v is the kinematic viscosity of the fluid.

5. The portion of the total undercooling consumed in driving the solute transport ΔT_S is given by:

$$\Delta T_S = T_L \; (C_\infty) - T_L(C_i) \tag{4e}$$

Because the growing crystal is small in size, has curved surfaces, and often contains nonequilibrium defects, the solid contains a higher free energy than the solid considered in generating a phase diagram that we use as our standard state in the overall treatment. Thus the equilibrium melting temperature for such a solid is lowered by an amount ΔT_E compared to that for the equilibrium solid. We find that the portion of the total undercooling consumed in the production of nonequilibrium solid ΔT_E can be expressed as

$$\Delta T_E = T_L \; (C_i) - T_E \; (C_i) = f_5 \; (\gamma, \, \Delta S, \, S^*, \Sigma_i, \, \gamma_i^f, \, \Sigma_i, \, N_i^f) \tag{4f}$$

where $T_E(C_i)$ is the equilibrium interface temperature for interface liquid concentration C_i, γ is the solid-liquid interfacial energy, ΔS is the entropy of fusion, γ_i^f is the fault energy for defects of type i, and N_i^f is the number of type i. (See Figure 7.)

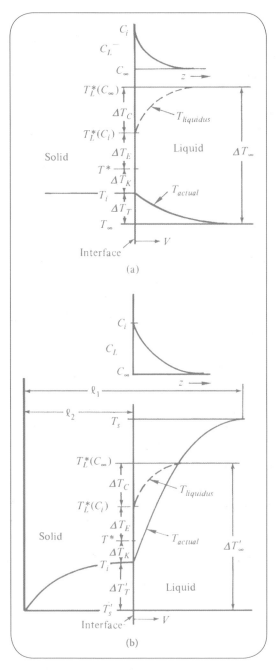

Figure 7: Solute and temperature distributions plus key temperatures for (a) unconstrained crystallization and (b) constrained crystallization.

6. Next, because the crystal is growing, a departure from the equilibrium temperature ΔT_K must exist at the interface in order to produce a net thermodynamic driving force for molecular attachment to the growing solid. At sufficiently large departures from equilibrium, the molecules can attach at any interface site and lower the free energy of the system. However, at small departures from equilibrium, molecular attachment at random interface sites generally leads to an increase in the free energy of the system; and thus, such interface attachment will not occur as a spontaneous process. Rather, in such an instance molecules become a part of the solid only by attachment at layer edge sites on the interface, and one must consider the various mechanisms of layer generation on the crystal surface. The portion of the total undercooling consumed in driving this interface process ΔT_K can be expressed as

$$\Delta T_K = T_E\,(C_i) - T_i = f_6\,(V,\, \mu_1,\, \mu_2,\, S^*,\, t) \qquad (4g)$$

where T_i is the actual interface temperature and where μ_1 and μ_2 are lumped parameters needed to specify the interface attachment kinetics for the various attachment mechanisms.

7. Finally, since the crystal is growing, it must be evolving latent heat and the interface temperature T_i must be sufficiently far above the bath temperature T_∞ to provide the potential for heat dissipation to the bath. That portion of the total undercooling consumed in driving the heat dissipation, ΔT_H, can be expressed as

$$\Delta T_H = T_i - T_\infty = f_7\,(K,\, \alpha,\, \Delta H,\, V,\, S^*,\, t) \qquad (4h)$$

where K refers to the thermal conductivity and α refers to the thermal diffusivity. The foregoing has been a description of the subdivision of the total bath undercooling, ΔT, into its four component parts, i.e.,

$$\Delta T = \Delta T_S + \Delta T_E + \Delta T_K + \Delta T_H \tag{4i}$$

Equation 4i is called the "coupling equation" and illustrates the fact that these four basic elements of physics enter every crystal growth situation and are intimately coupled through this constraint. However, for different materials, certain components of Equation 4i tend to dominate the phase transformation. In the growth of metal crystals from a relatively pure melt, $\Delta T_H \sim \Delta T$ so that this case is largely controlled by heat flow. During the growth of an oxide crystal from a melt of steel, e.g., $\Delta T_S \sim \Delta T$, so that the growth is largely diffusion-controlled. During the growth of a polymer crystal from a well-fractionated polymeric melt, $\Delta T_K \sim \Delta T$ and the growth is largely controlled by the kinetics of interface attachment. Finally, during the growth of a lamellar eutectic crystal, $\Delta T_E \sim \Delta T/2$ and the growth is to a large degree controlled by the excess free energy of the solid (due to the formation of α/ß phase boundaries).

By considering Figure 8, which is a plot of crystal growth velocity as a function of time, we find that at small times ΔT_E in Equation 4i dominates the crystal's growth and thus plays an overriding role in its initial morphology.

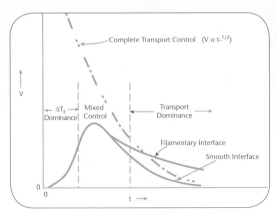

Figure 8: Schematic of particle growth velocity V versus time t, illustrating the regions where various mechanisms are dominant.

At large times ΔT_S and ΔT_H in Equation 4i dominate the crystal's growth and lead to very different morphologies. At intermediate times all four factors play significant roles in the shape adopted by the crystal.

There is little doubt that crystal morphology plays a significant role in the resultant crystal perfection, and that this morphology is largely determined by the subtle interplay of the factors already discussed. However, the prediction of crystal shape with time is a problem that only recently can be solved in any general way. This arises because the problem thus far stated is, in general, not completely specified. Knowing V and S*, C_i and T_i can be completely determined in terms of C_∞ and T_∞, respectively; and ΔT_S, ΔT_E, ΔT_K, and ΔT_H are completely determined in the general mathematical sense. However, we don't know either V or S*. If S*(t) is specified, Equation 4i can be used to determine V(t). We are in need of an additional condition to completely specify the problem and thus provide simultaneous prediction of both V(S) and S*(t).

We shall find that our extra condition is generated by considering the response of the growing crystal to shape perturbations. It can be easily shown that the various elements of the interface will always be subjected to fluctuations in ΔT and in its component ΔT_i's. Thus, given sufficient time we should always expect that shape distortions will have a finite probability of forming on the crystal surface and that the crystal will evolve to that shape which is most stable in the environment that allows such perturbations. With the addition of our perturbation response equation in the general form

$$\mathbf{V^*(S) = f_8 \ (S^*, \ \Delta T_S, \ \Delta T_E, \ \Delta T_K, \ \Delta T_H)} \qquad (4j)$$

the most stable crystal shape, S*, and the corresponding growth velocity at various points on the crystal surface, V*, may be evaluated from equations 4i and 4j. From the experimental side of the picture, unconstrained crystallization of water containing various solutes has been well studied via the conventional variables since the late 1950s with cinemaphotography used to see the ice-crystal morphological changes depending on the variable changes invoked. In particular, the entire range of crystal morphologies shown in reference 6 has been observed for constant ΔT and $\dot{T}$ by adjusting both the concentration and type of added solute and ΔT_C, the undercooling at which the ice-crystal nucleation is initiated. Thus, one can conclude that, in reference 6, one is dealing with the normal crystallization process perturbed perhaps somewhat by the human consciousness invoked.

In the first section of this chapter, our IIED-experiments clearly confirmed robust effects of human intention on various processes of physical reality. Some of this psychoenergetic effect has been shown to be directly correlated with the raising of the thermodynamic free-energy state of the system when the two unique levels of physical reality, P_1 and P_2, become significantly coupled together. In addition, a quantitative measure of this change has been demonstrated using an H^+ ion probe.[14] If such a coupled system was generated in the Emoto experiments, then this would alter the thermodynamic driving force, ΔG, up or down for the water-crystallization process; and one could expect significant changes thereby. However, before jumping to such a conclusion, there is an experimental difficulty that first must be resolved.

In the Emoto experimental protocol,[6] one starts with a cold chamber at $0°C - \Delta T_\infty$ where ΔT_∞ is presumed to be sufficiently large that most if not all of his water samples are well below their liquidus temperature and thus should eventually freeze. However, one can't be completely sure of this because he doesn't specify C_∞ and the solute type/types. Nevertheless, let us presume that ΔT_∞ is sufficiently large that ΔT_∞ is greater than $\{0°C - \Delta T_\infty (C_\infty) - \Delta T_C\}$ so his samples will all freeze. Let us suppose that he uses a tray with 25 water-sample holders at room temperature well above $0°C$ and places them into his cold chamber. The water samples will begin to lose heat to the chamber so they cool at a rate $\dot{T}$, which slows down with time. At a melt undercooling of ΔT_C, they begin to nucleate ice crystals, probably on the top surface of the water (because the heat transfer rate is greatest there). These small crystals will float, because water expands upon freezing; and the value of N_0 becomes important here in determining the ultimate crystal size and perfection. To determine if there is a significant correlation between ice-crystal morphology and a written intention message pasted on the tray, one would need to see more than 20 of the 25 cups providing the same crystal morphology, and in a repeatable way. If this level of replicability or better isn't achieved, one shouldn't take the result to be a very significant one. As a more refined experiment, one should start with purified water and add a specific solute to a concentration, C_∞, and let this be the sample water for the written messages. In addition, between uses, the sample tray should be heated to a temperature well above room temperature and vacuum dried so that all previous ice fragments are removed from microscopic crevasses in the tray.

CONCLUSIONS

1. Information is the connecting bridge between energy and all forms of consciousness.

2. Experiments associated with IIED conditioning of laboratory spaces have led to the discovery of a second unique level of physical reality beyond our normal electric atom/molecule level of physical reality.

3. Experiments carried out in an IIED-conditioned space allow digital measuring instruments to gain accessibility to this new magnetic vacuum information wave domain, so that any material property measurement magnitude is now given by Equation 2 of the text.

4. If α_{eff} in Equation 2 is negligible, then these two domains of physical reality are uncoupled so the property magnitude is unchanged from that given by standard experimentation in an "unconditioned" space. If α_{eff} is of significant magnitude ($\sim 0.1 < \alpha_{eff} < 1$), then applied human consciousness can modulate a physical property magnitude

either upwards or downwards relative to that observed for an "unconditioned" space.

5. The human acupuncture meridian/chakra system is experimentally found to be at the same EM symmetry state as an IIED-conditioned space, so focused human intent can either temporarily or continuously increase the magnitude of $\propto_{eff}$ into the significant range.

6. Standard science of crystallization theory for our normal electric atom/molecule level of physical reality shows that all ice-crystal morphologies displayed in the Emoto research have been reproduced earlier by others.

7. For similar research carried out in an IIED-conditioned space, a new, additional, contribution labeled "the magnetoelectrochemical potential contribution" needs to be added to the thermodynamic free-energy driving force, ΔG, for the water-to-ice phase transition, which will, in turn, alter the form of the dominant ice-crystal morphology observed during this phase transition.

8. This author has not yet seen in the Emoto research clear proof of a strong correlation between a written intention statement and specific ice-crystal morphology result.

○ ○ ○

REFERENCES

1. C. E. Shannon, "A mathematical theory of communication," *The Bell System Technical Journal* 27, (1948): pp. 379–423 (July) and 623–56 (October).

2. L. Brillouin, *Science and Information Theory,* second edition, New York, NY: Academic Press, 1962: Chapter 12.

3. L. Brillouin, *Scientific Uncertainty and Information,* New York, NY: Academic Press, 1964: Chapter 1.

4. J. E. and M. G. Mayer, *Statistical Mechanics,* New York, NY: John Wiley & Sons, Inc., 1940: pp.105–106.

5. J. W. Gibbs, *The Collected Works of J. Willard Gibbs,* New Haven, CT: Yale University Press, 1957, volumes I and II.

6. M. Emoto, *The Message from Water,* Tokyo: HADO Kyoikusha, 2002.

7. W. A. Tiller, *Science and Human Transformation: Subtle Energies, Intentionality, and Consciousness,* Walnut Creek, CA: Pavior Publishing, 1997.

8. W. A. Tiller; W. E. Dibble, Jr.; and M. J. Kohane, *Conscious Acts of Creation: The Emergence of a New Physics,* Walnut Creek, CA: Pavior Publishing, 2001.

9. W. A. Tiller; W. E. Dibble, Jr; and J. G. Fandel, *Some Science Adventures with Real Magic,* Walnut Creek, CA: Pavior Publishing, 2005.

10. R. M. Eisberg, *Fundamentals of Modern Physics,* New York, NY: John Wiley and Sons, 1961: pp 140–6.

11. W. A. Tiller, "Dendrites: Understanding of this familiar phenomenon has led to the development of useful man-made materials," *Science* 146, no. 3646 (1964): p. 871.

12. W. A. Tiller, *The Science of Crystallization: Microscopic Interface Phenomena,* Cambridge: Cambridge University Press, 1991.

13. W. A. Tiller, *Macroscopic Phenomena and Defect Generation,* Cambridge: Cambridge University Press, 1991.

14. W. A. Tiller and W. E. Dibble, Jr., "Towards general experimentation and discovery in 'conditioned' laboratory spaces, part V: data on ten different sites using a new type of detector," to be published in the *Journal of Alternative and Complementary Medicine,* 2006.

◊◊◊ ◊◊◊

CHAPTER 2

THE STRUCTURE OF LIQUID WATER: ITS RELEVANCE TO HOMEOPATHY, ULTRADILUTE SOLS (OR COLLOIDS), AND IMPRINTED WATERS

by Rustum Roy

ABSTRACT

Water is the single most important material for the existence and support of human life and health. It has been almost totally neglected by post–World War II biochemical medicine, in spite of the latter's incredibly generous research budgets. The signal failure of such research—as demonstrated daily in its outcome statistics and the U.S. health-care system's unenviable track record as the leading vector of death among all illnesses—is in no small measure due to the peculiar shortsighted focus on organic biochemistry, which has no place in the study of the role of water in human health.

This unique relationship—water and health—has been emphasized in many concrete and symbolic ways in virtually every ancient tradition. The scientific study of water has been carried out so far by the chemistry community, with an approach emphasizing the molecular level of structure. According to a recent major review, physicists and materials scientists find water to exist in a nearly infinite set of structures, which are uniquely labile, changeable among themselves.

The core argument of this paper is that the materials-science literature establishes that common highly covalent liquids, including water, exist in many, many very different structures, even thermodynamically stable ones. The paper establishes the *plausibility* of causing structural changes in water—imprinting it, so to speak—by many common vectors, which include not only temperature and pressure, but also epitaxy, succussing, electric and magnetic fields, and the like, and possibly human intention. Among these are three specific vectors used in the preparation of homeopathic remedies:

1. Epitaxy, a phenomenon very little known even by scientists but used daily worldwide in materials technologies, which involves the transference of structural information (not any composition whatsoever) from one solid (or liquid) to a liquid

2. Succussing, which can generate substantial pressures that are known to change the structure of similar liquids

3. The creation of nanobubbles, which would be distributed as in a colloid (like milk) and definitely change the structure

This argument demolishes the 150-year-old argument used against homeopathy—that since the compositional dilution is beyond the Avogadro limit and has excluded any of the original molecules of the additives, there can be no difference between the succussed remedy and the original water. Water *can* be changed in structure without any change in composition.

INTRODUCTION

The entire field of water-structure research by scientists—so far, conducted essentially only by chemists—has focused largely on its composition and, within that, the composition and structure of "molecules" or small oligomers, and often not even on *liquid* water at all. There has been almost no state-of-the-art research on the 3-D structure or arrangement of the units in space. This has resulted in a neglect of the most directly connected science of (inorganic) materials and physics. In addition, of course, insofar as the structure of water relates to human health, it has also led to the total exclusion of the human mind and spirit (an absolute part of the reality of a whole person).

A new and comprehensive view of the structure of water from the materials-science perspective was published only in December 2005 by Roy, Bell, Tiller, and Hoover (RBTH). This paper is the major source of data for this essay and contains dozens of useful references to which the reader is referred. This essay attempts to point out the links, in less technical terms than that paper, to various procedures or interventions involving water in whole-person healing. It does not provide any research or data to validate any particular approach or healing procedure related to water.

HOW THIS REDUCTIONIST SCIENCE FITS INTO THE WHOLIST PERSPECTIVE OF THIS BOOK

This book is concerned with a vast range of observations on healing by various procedures, agencies, practices, and so on—especially those involving water. Regrettably, in an era dominated by fundamentalism (defined very accurately simply as the conviction that *only my way* leads to truth), some in the scientific community have taken on the coloration of the religious fundamentalists whom they vigorously oppose. But science is the very antithesis of a guarantee of the permanent truth of our *current* views. Its accurate motto is, of course, that taken from the Protestant Reformation: *semper reformanda* ("always changing"). As scientists, we *know* that our truth may always be improved upon or incorporated into a larger truth with some new discovery. Indeed, every topflight scientist hopes to achieve exactly that: to replace or improve a major paradigm by their new insights.

Let me start by citing my own experience to show how pervasive within communities of science—much closer to the heartland of real science than statistical medicine—this proto-fundamentalism is. In the late 1940s, my department head in geosciences at Penn State warned me not to be misled by the American geological establishment. This entire body, he warned me, had rejected Alfred Wegener's nearly 20-year-old proposal of continental drift. With all the fervor of Southern preachers, the gurus of American geoscience derided Wegener's view as absurd. Yet, slowly but surely, over a decade or two, their views were totally washed away by the tidal wave of more and more facts. Without any fanfare or public mea culpa, one "certainly correct" theory was abandoned and another one installed! Scientific "truth" changes, and true scientists worldwide celebrate its ability to do so.

Here's another example: Within the next decade, the controversy was all about the volcanoes on the moon. When my graduate student Frank Dachille wrote a rather simple, rambling book, *Target Earth,* proposing that the moon was actually pockmarked not by volcanoes but by craters caused by meteor impact, I was advised by leaders of the nation's major geological professional society to dismiss him from the university! Such a believer in the absurd, they advised me, should not be allowed to get a degree, even though his research with me was totally unrelated to the moon. Ten years later, meteorite impacts on both moon and Earth were a very hot research topic of—yes, the very same orthodox scientists. *Sic transit!*

One community within science, inorganic chemistry, has monopolized the study of the "structure" of water. The biomolecular medical establishment has paid no attention to it. Hence essentially zero scientific work has been done on healing and water by the conventional medical establishment. On the other hand, those intimately involved with human beings in healing—such as Florence Nightingale with her insistence on cleanliness and washing, and Hahnemann and his nearly pure water remedies—have had profound effects on large populations, even on the medical establishment in the case of Nightingale! Today, it's finally possible to revive more objectively the question of the efficacy of various water-based healing vectors suggested by traditional practices.

In my 60 years of work at the cutting edge of materials science, I've always worked with one common approach: Find the most interesting observations, "wild facts," as William James called them, or "useful truths," in the words of Ben Franklin (see the Bibliography), which are unexplainable by current theories and hence spurned by almost all scientists. Go after those areas. I did, and I ran across several key data that had this in common: They were all involved with water.

I'll start here with the most provable data, testable by normal medical procedures: the extraordinary antibacterial (and antiviral) effects obtained with ultradilute metallic sols (or colloids), especially of silver. A sol is merely a permanent suspension, just like, say, milk, of very fine particles of a different solid or liquid. For anyone advocating the possibility of producing profound health effects with (essentially) pure water, the easy demonstration of such effects is the use of such a silver sol or colloid (easily found in any health-food store) made up of roughly 1 ppm (or one part per million atomic concentration) of metallic particles in the 10 nm range. This is the best proof or "existence theorem" for attention-focusing by the less informed. In any assemblage of petri dishes containing the usual range of test bacteria, the antibacterial effects of these ultradilute sols can be demonstrated in minutes and compare favorably with the best antibiotics. How can essentially pure water do this?

The range of these effects has been and is being demonstrated worldwide, most relevantly these days in the battlefields of Iraq and Afghanistan. This remarkable fact is never reported in the mass media. Most startling to this author is the connection of this water and silver and electric current to some of the most significant medical issues today: the regeneration of human limbs (fingertips), as demonstrated by Becker and Flick many years ago.

If a sol of silver at a 1 ppm concentration can do this, can the structure of different spa waters, and hence their health effects, be different because of the influence of the structurally different suspended particulate colloidal mineral matter? Can radiation—whether electric fields from megavolt overhead wires or microwave magnetic fields—change and even leave an imprint on water?

Detailed scientific papers from Japan present data on just such possibilities. In contrast with the multitrillion–dollar sales power of the pharmaceutical industry and a $30 billion annual research budget for National Intstitutes of Health (NIH) alone, however, the research in this area receives essentially zero funding.

It will be seen in the RBTH paper that there is no doubt whatsoever that water near our ambient conditions has several different structures. By far the biggest of the scientific issues remaining concerns the *kinetics of change* of one such structure or large cluster to another.

THE ABSOLUTE IMPORTANCE OF "STRUCTURE"

This book is about the relation of water to human healing. Water is the largest component of the human body. But what is it about this liquid that can make it a healing vector?

First, of course, water, being the amazing solvent that it is (because of its extraordinarily high dielectric constant), does take into solution a great deal of the other materials that come into contact with it. This fact has tended to emphasize the composition—the "purity," if you will—of the water as its most important descriptor. *That's the problem.* Composition, especially slight changes of it, is rarely important in altering the properties of a liquid or solid. One reason is that all such variations are incremental, continuous, and slight. But changes in structure can be dramatic. One example will do to make my point: The element carbon exists in many solid forms, including graphite and diamond, meaning that the nearly softest and the hardest (so far) materials on the planet have an identical composition. Here we have *exactly* the same composition of matter, easily transformed from one structure—in milliseconds—to the other, with this incredible difference in properties. So if you're interested in water, you'll have to pay attention to its *structure.*

The paper and this essay start by distinguishing the way materials scientists and chemists define the term *structure.*

Essentially, all previous literature on water structure has been dominated by chemists, who equate the term with the identification of the *molecular species* present in the vapor, in the liquid, at its surface, or in some specific environment. Literally dozens of such molecular species have been identified, calculated, or inferred. For hundreds of precise illustrations of proposed structures of the H_2O molecule and the assumed dimers, trimers tetramers, and on and on, the gold standard of references is the Website maintained by Professor Martin Chaplin in London (see Bibliography).

Since nearly 100 percent of the literature deals with the size and shape of the *building blocks* of the condensed matter (liquid), what's studied very little is the materials scientist's approach to the structure of condensed matter—the *arrangement* of these building blocks in 3-D space. The two views can be sharply distinguished by using this analogy: Consider the radical differences between the structure of *the building blocks* and *the building itself.* One doesn't describe the structure of Notre Dame or the Taj Mahal by saying that they consist of limestone, sandstone, or marble blocks and giving details of the size and shape of these blocks. We know that the structure of these buildings is of the whole, not of the parts. Or consider the pieces or blocks in a Lego set (= molecules) (the chemists' approach) and the "structure" of the house or car or plane (= clusters) that a child builds with the same blocks.

This materials-science approach to the structure of a liquid— any liquid of course—is extremely difficult here, simply because water is a liquid. That means that the units or building blocks do not repeat in any periodic manner in their 3-D arrangement. This periodic-arrangement state is the property of virtually all of Earth's inorganic matter—99.99 percent of it! The units are crystalline. The aperiodic state—the *noncrystalline state,* also called, imprecisely, the "glassy state"—which is the common structure of *all* liquids, poses a nearly insuperable barrier to the main scientific tools for determining structure—all the diffraction methods, x-ray, electrons, neutrons—and water's low viscosity doesn't help. Of course there are other techniques—spectroscopies of all kinds—but they are poor substitutes for diffraction. Also, there are enormous resources available by analogy from the extensive 100-year research on the structure of glasses and other liquidlike phases, especially those of SiO_2, with its close similarity to H_2O. The nearly ubiquitous structural heterogeneity in similar covalently bonded *liquids*, even of *elements* (such as S, Se, Te, and the like), is also a major hint of the possibilities for a variety of structures in water, however long they last.

Very useful lessons can be learned about the structure of water from the enormous literature on SiO_2 and silicate minerals and glasses. These are slowly being rediscovered. The first major learning is that most common glasses are highly heterogeneous in structure, consisting of 5–50 nm clusters with different structures. Another little-known example is the effect of pressure on liquid structures such as the thoroughly studied SiO_2-glass, which shows the change of properties and structures with pressure in SiO_2 and related glasses. (These data are largely from my own laboratories in the 1960s and 1970s and the references are all in the Roy, Bell, Tiller, Hoover 2005 paper.)

In the same vein, by the 1980s the most experienced analysts of the structure of glasses had concluded that they nearly all exhibited a mixture of different structures at the few nanometer level. Most glasses—especially those containing SiO_2, with its close similarity to H_2O—therefore were nanoheterogeneous, consisting of islands of different structure. Glassy water exhibits a whole range of properties very similar to glassy silicates. There is little reason, therefore, to doubt that liquid water carries at least some of the vestiges of this fundamental nanoheterogeneity.

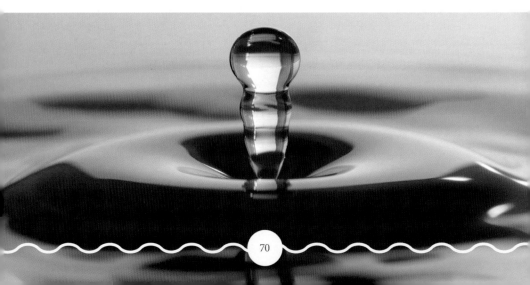

THE KEY ARGUMENT LINKING
STRUCTURE TO HEALTH VECTORS

What's presented here simply points out the unchallenged fact that the criticism—nay, ridicule—heaped on homeopathy and "structured" water by chemists is, in fact, itself based on an egregious error caused by a simplistic understanding of the properties of liquids. The critics' argument is, in sum total: The only way to change the properties of water is to add some solute. It is assumed that water can only be changed by controlling the nature and concentration of the solute. This is, of course, sheer heresy to materials scientists, and known to be inaccurate by all informed scientists. The central principle of materials science is that properties are determined largely by *structure* (at every level, from nano to macro) and *not composition,* as described above and illustrated by the diamond/graphite example. This phenomenon is true of virtually all solids, though not with such spectacular differences as diamond and graphite.

EFFECTING STRUCTURAL CHANGE

We have thus disposed of the 200-year-old mistaken argument; it remains only to establish that even in H_2O it's possible and plausible that such structural changes can be effected. That's what the Roy, Bell, Tiller, Hoover paper attempts. It makes no contribution at all to whether or not homeopathic or ultradilute sol remedies work in the clinic or not.

Three well-known phenomena in materials research are utilized to demonstrate the plausibility of structural change in water: (1) epitaxy, (2) pressure, and (3) nanobubbles.

EPITAXY

A key insight from common experience in materials science

that may be relevant to understanding the structure of water and what can affect it easily is "epitaxy." This term doesn't appear even in most technical dictionaries, but the phenomenon is very well known, studied, and used in dozens of everyday technologies in materials science. Yet, besides the plausible differences in nanostructure, it has *never* been invoked directly in the literature on the various healing traditions, including homeopathy, or in the use of different healing spas, which may have waters with *suspended* (not in solution) mineral matter.

Epitaxy is the transmission of structural information from the surface (hence *epi*) of one material (usually a solid) to another (usually a liquid). Subtleties of terminology appear in various papers, but it's the template of the structure—that is, the information—that's definitely transferred. Recent examples of the subtleties of information that can be so transferred can be found in the literature cited at the end of this essay. *No matter* is transferred in this "imprinting." Hence, the traditional hackneyed criticism of homeopathy—the discussions of "concentrations of solutes above or below Avogadro's limit"—are totally irrelevant. By providing a specific structure as a template (usually solid but sometimes liquid), one can induce an entire body of liquid to precipitate or crystallize in that preselected structure or morphology. The seeding of clouds is caused by epitaxial growth of crystalline ice or water on a substrate of AgI, which has the same crystal structure. Seeding and epitaxial growth of semiconductors are universally practiced in major modern technology. Information and "memory" are transmitted from the seed or substrate to the liquid phase, which can completely control the structure of what's formed from it. No chemical transfer whatsoever occurs.

In homeopathy, a specific active agent is added to the liquid (water or water + ethanol). The relevant question is, in what ways can the active agent change, affect, or imprint the liquid? Those unfamiliar with materials science assume that it is only by its presence in solution (as atoms, ions, or molecules) that an "active agent" can affect a liquid. They're wrong. Here again we return to the *structure,* not the *composition,* for explanations. Obviously, the structure of water *can* be influenced by that of solids with which it's in contact.

These, then, are the first well-established learnings from materials science—structural nanoheterogeneity within liquids and the role of epitaxy in propagating structural information without involving composition. In addition to the above, materials scientists deal extensively with other phenomena which are certainly possible, and probably major, factors in the structure of water.

SUCCUSSING: CREATING HIGH PRESSURES AND NANOBUBBLES

Pressure, after temperature, is of course the most important of the intensive thermodynamic variables in deciding what structure is stable and/or will form. Pressure is well known to have profound effects on crystalline H_2O. Some 13 different crystalline H_2O structures are known in modest p-t space. In a series of papers in the 1960s, we've already shown that it's well known that all glasses (frozen liquids) change structure (and their density and refractive index properties) continuously with pressure. Such densified structures survive easily in the oxides studied, which are much more viscous. A reasonable extrapolation will show that under the "normal" succussing procedures, very respectable pressures (say in the 10 kbar range) will be generated on the very small size water droplets that must form. Reasoning from analogy with similar (that is, covalent) liquids, there will, quite reasonably, be many different structures of water formed both by pressures generated in succussing and possibly others in some combination with the epitaxy on any additives.

Finally, the succussing process must necessarily also produce a range of sizes of bubbles in the liquid. The size distribution of the bubbles will certainly include some nanobubbles—that is, nanosize inclusions of gaseous O_2, N_2, CO_2, possibly the active ingredient, and so on. Some of these bubble sizes will no doubt be well below the colloid range, and therefore a colloidal suspension of water +

gaseous (or liquid) inclusions would be formed. These could be quite stable for very long periods and would certainly affect the structure of the liquid water.

OTHER VARIABLES RELEVANT
TO STRUCTURED WATERS AND SOLS

In addition to these major important variables, which can affect the stability and determine the structure of water, there are the other very common variables: magnetic and electric fields. While such fields contribute very little to the stability of most materials, they become profoundly important when these effects can interact with or be "locked into" a material in, for example, ordered domains or regions that are present in very common ferroelectric or ferromagnetic materials. Indeed, our own very recent work has demonstrated the most spectacular changes in, and even destruction of, the crystal structures of common inorganic phases by magnetic fields of a few gauss at microwave frequencies (see Bibliography). These results were totally unexpected and are still unexplained by the world's leading theorists.

MATERIALS SCIENCE DATA
FROM HOMEOPATHIC LITERATURE

These data and insights from the physical sciences are followed by the increasing data from several researchers in the homeopathic literature, adducing evidence on the effects of various materials-science variables, including weak magnetic fields, which fit very well with our models.

The book by Bellavite and Signorini (see Bibliography) summarizes much of their own work and that of others who have already approached the same problem from the stance of homeopathy. Various investigators have previously proposed a model for the structure of water involving formation of aggregates of water molecules or water clusters, possibly seeded by—but not requiring—the continued presence of molecules from the original source substance (for example, zwitterions or clathrates). Others have proposed the involvement of a coherent electromagnetic radiation field within the solvent that contributes order to the molecular motion. Emerging data on the structure and thermodynamics of water provide a rationale for revisiting the role of the solvent in storing and transmitting the information of homeopathy-prepared agents. The reader is referred again to the paper to avoid overloading on jargon.

SUMMARY OF THE CURRENT VIEW OF THE STRUCTURE OF WATER

The short description of the structure of water that emerges today is that H_2O liquid is indeed a nanoheterogenous statistical-mechanical distribution mainly of several molecular species including both oligomers and polymers and a minority of monomers. The structure is easily affected by epitaxial effects, pressure during succussing, and also the formation of colloidal nanobubbles. This distribution is very labile; and all the intensive and extensive variables, including magnetic and electric fields, can cause substantial changes in the distribution, and hence the structure, and hence the properties. In simple terms: Liquid water consists of a changing aggregate of islands of different size and shape in an arrangement that can easily be changed.

CONNECTIONS TO HUMAN INTENTION ON HEALING

So, finally, what of the possible effects of human intention on water, such as those of Dr. Emoto? The huge amount of solid data on the amazing reality and importance of the expectation effects (EE) (inaccurately labeled by the mystifying and wholly unnecessary term "placebo") in *all* human healing transactions, including the highest high-tech procedures, certainly entitles any scientist to hypothesize about the possibility of various modes of human-intention effects on healing.

Dr. Emoto's work appears to confirm this possibility in a graphically attractive way, as does Stephan Schwartz's work on water in healer's hands using I-R spectroscopy. The Qi Gong master Dr. Yan Xin's classic demonstration of the change of the structure of water as measured in a Raman spectrometer from a distance of hundreds of meters to 7,000 kilometers is part of this database. With the amassing of a wide range of data from different fields, it's certainly fair to conclude that our understanding of the healing potential of water is, to use the title of a book by the really great physician-healer Lewis Thomas, today's *Youngest Science.* We know it has a bright future. What we need now is to pursue it—carefully, bearing in mind the power of human intention, and with the goal of fairness.

○ ○ ○

BIBLIOGRAPHY

P. Bellavite and A. Signorini, *The Emerging Science of Homeopathy: Complexity, Biodynamics, and Nanopharmacology,* second edition, Berkeley, CA: North Atlantic Books, 2002.

Martin Chaplin's Website: **www.martin.chaplin.btinternet. co.uk**

R. Roy, I. R. Bell, W. A. Tiller, and R. Hoover, "The structure of liquid water: novel insight from materials research; potential relevance to homeopathy," *Materials Research Innovations,* no. 9 (2005), issue 4: pp.78–103.

○ ○ ○   ○ ○ ○

CHAPTER 3

WATER: ITS CLINICAL AND SCIENTIFIC DEPTHS

by Cyril W. Smith

SUMMARY

Coming from a background in radar and physics, and while working on electromagnetic effects in enzymes and living systems, I became involved in the diagnosis and therapy of patients hypersensitive to their electromagnetic environment. This led to research on the physics of water, its memory for frequencies, and the use of dowsing as a scientific instrument; the results led to a basis for homeopathy and acupuncture. Frequency was the relevant parameter throughout. Acupuncture meridians have characteristic frequencies naturally present on them. Where there's a connection to the autonomic nervous system (ANS), additional frequencies characteristic of the ANS appear. The presence of these frequencies in the whole body field of a person indicates which systems are under stress. A study of techniques for writing, reading, and erasing frequencies in water gave results of practical value. Logic-gate operations with frequency were shown to be possible in spatial arrangements of water and sensitive enough for nerve impulse trains to control biocomputing. Theoretical work cited predicts domains of phase coherence as a normal property of water. Measurements involving these suggest that the Emoto ice-crystal patterns may start on coherence domains and indicate frequency patterns within.

INTRODUCTION

Since 1973, I've been involved in experimental research on the interactions of electromagnetic fields with biomaterials and living systems. This included my cooperation with the late Professor Herbert Fröhlich, FRS, a theoretical physicist at Liverpool University whose centenary was celebrated recently. One early conclusion from this work was that there were unusual magnetic field effects in water and in living biological systems and that these were only explicable in terms of 20th-century physics, not 19th-century physics. These effects involved highly complex systems that could become interconnected through sharing frequencies that had become synchronized in phase (that is, become coherent). This could happen over distances that might span many molecules; but, as we were dealing with quantum systems, distance might be an irrelevance.

HYPERSENSITIVE PATIENTS

My involvement in the diagnosis and therapy of patients hypersensitive to their electromagnetic environment began in 1982 at the request of Dr. Jean Monro in London. Working with her electrically hypersensitive patients and those of Dr. W. J. Rea in Dallas, Texas, gave me an insight into the extremes of sensitivity and speeds of reaction of hypersensitive patients whose regulatory systems had failed, particularly when they were exposed to electromagnetic fields and frequencies.

Such patients have a long history of ongoing hypersensitivities to many chemicals and/or foods and particulates. They may react within seconds to something in their surroundings to which they happen to be hypersensitive. This includes their electromagnetic environment; and here, frequency is the important factor. Any frequency (from circadian rhythms to light) may be clinically significant.

One important result from this clinical work was finding that the effects on patients of environmental electromagnetic fields, chemicals, or homeopathic potencies could be reproduced with frequency-imprinted water. For example, water in flame-sealed glass ampoules was imprinted with frequencies through the glass with no possibility of any chemical contamination. Patients reacted to this even if the water was frozen. This showed us that the basis of homeopathy must be frequencies in water.

The frequencies that affect these patients are often those that occur naturally on the acupuncture meridians. These are rather like microwave links running through the body originating as coherence between adjacent cells in the embryo. Enough water remains in a specimen of a tissue even after staining and fixing as a microscope slide for frequency measurements to be made, and these correlate well with the natural frequencies found on the acupuncture meridians (and chakras) regarded by Traditional Chinese Medicine as connecting to these organs. Chemicals (except 100 percent halogen-saturated ones) have a characteristic frequency signature resulting from their interaction with traces of hydrogen-bonded water.

THEORETICAL

Preparata and Del Giudice at the University of Milan did a theoretical investigation of the properties of coherence in condensed matter—which is anything that's not a gas. Their model for water is the same as for all other coherent condensed-matter systems. Namely, there are two parts: one *incoherent,* comprising water molecules oscillating at random (as in steam, but more densely packed); and the other *coherent,* consisting of domains of *coherence,* within which all the water molecules oscillate synchronously (in phase) with the frequency of a very large electromagnetic field that develops spontaneously within the domain. This resembles what happens in the laser, but it doesn't need any energy "pumping." Predictions from their theory are in good agreement with the experimentally determined values for physical constants of liquid water.

The "classical electromagnetic field" is the basis of electronics and radio; it describes oscillations whose phase is well defined (coherent) but for which the number of particles (quanta, photons) carrying the energy is undefined. A "quantum field" has uncertainty in both its phase and the number of particles involved, and this uncertainty is determined by the Heisenberg Relation. The more the uncertainty is taken up by fluctuation in the number of particles, the more perfect the phase coherence becomes.

For any wave, its velocity of propagation equals its frequency multiplied by its wavelength. Within a coherent system such as water, the range of the coherence (coherence length) becomes the constant quantity instead of the velocity. This makes frequency proportional to velocity apparently without restriction, so long as one remains within the coherence length. Such a system can support many velocities (even greater than the velocity of light) with frequencies in proportion; and because these no longer have absolute values, the system has become *fractal*. The same patterns and effects can occur in many different parts of the electromagnetic spectrum. It's this that connects frequencies characteristic of chemical, technical, and biological systems together. If there weren't a duality between the chemical bond and frequencies, spectroscopic analysis would be impossible. This is why a pattern of frequencies can mimic a chemical exposure for hypersensitive patients and trigger their reactions.

IMPRINTING, READING, AND ERASING

Clinically significant information can be imprinted into a vial of water by *succussion,* which is sharply banging it on a surface. This is what creates a homeopathic *potency.* Frequency information from a patient's body can be collected similarly, and this often reveals stress on acupuncture meridians.

IMPRINTING

Imprinting can occur through the glass of a vial containing water by immersing it in frequency-imprinted water. Otherwise, water placed near a source of frequencies (an oscillator and coil, or a chemical or a potency) can be imprinted by a strong magnet or a toroid (ring) of a ferrite material. A sequence of seven voltage pulses will also make an imprint; a mobile phone may do this on dial-up.

READING

William Tiller has described work with memory chips imprinted by healers. Although healing can be imprinted, it is also possible to imprint stress. When I visited the laboratory of Jacques Benveniste shortly after the *Nature* inquisition had left, I was able to find by dowsing all the glassware (in a box on the top shelf of the store), the bench, and the incubator that had been used through the stress left behind. It's easy for a person who has the capability of a healer and knows how to do so to affect sensitive living systems such as those Benveniste was using. I told him to trash everything or treat it as if contaminated with radioactivity in order to get his laboratory clean again.

I've shown that the basic arithmetical operations can be performed on frequencies imprinted into water and that the basic reversible logic gates and their operations can be implemented. Nerve impulses should be able to control computing operations in living systems, making biocomputing a possibility.

ERASING

A water imprint is erased by briefly shielding it from the Earth's (geomagnetic) field, such as by placing it inside a steel box. Heating imprinted water alters the imprint, which may become "hidden." It can be recovered by the application of certain frequencies, which include those of the heart acupuncture meridian and chakra. The heart meridian frequency is on the Schumann Band, a geophysical resonance in the upper atmosphere under which life evolved. Another such frequency is the microwave resonance of molecular hydrogen. Medications can be made acceptable to sensitive patients by canceling their chemical signatures.

WATER'S FREQUENCY MEMORY

Frequencies in water and living systems present a very great measurement problem. Clinically, they may be anywhere in the electromagnetic spectrum. These aren't frequencies of "classical" electric or magnetic fields, but rather frequencies of "quantum" fields, which must be converted to the former for measurement with instruments. Information is carried as the frequency of the A-field component, which was originally a mathematical necessity arising from the fact that a magnetic field was found in closed loops. Eventually, it was shown theoretically by Aharanov and Bohm and later experimentally that this component of the magnetic field (called the magnetic vector potential) did actually exist and could produce interference effects.

DOWSING

To measure frequencies in water, I had to develop the dowsing techniques I'd initially devised for the diagnosis of reactions in very hypersensitive patients—persons incompatible with technology, period! This was the only technique able to cover the frequency range and sensitivity required. I later extended it to the detection of resonances in water, allergen dilutions, and homeopathic potencies. I've detected the frequency signature of salt (sodium chloride) to a concentration of about 0.3 ppm by weight in water.

My dowsing measurements agree with instrumentation where this has been possible. Their internal consistency is good.

Mind-body interactions make "double-blinding" difficult, if not impossible. The dowsing reaction must involve the heart or pericardium acupuncture meridians; if either is joined to a wire, all dowsing response is lost. A magnetic $\underline{A}$-field reverses the dowsing response as it does for the Aharanov-Bohm effect. Since a frequency can be measured in less than the time for a single cycle, its measurement must involve a phase comparison between the left and right arms. (See also Chapter 8.)

FREQUENCY MEASUREMENTS

There are several possibilities for objective frequency measurements. Electrodes immersed in water and connected to the input of a very sensitive amplifier or signal analyzer can detect an imprinted frequency in the kilohertz region if the water is excited by that frequency. A possible physical mechanism for this is that charges entering coherent water from an electrode must do so as charge-pairs; this reduces the number of charges at the water/electrode interface, thereby increasing the electrical resistance. The small "offset" current that flows into an amplifier detects this as a voltage.

Gariaev, in Moscow, has developed a special laser in which two beams are polarized perpendicular to each other. The beams interact with molecular structures, which produce optical rotation, resulting in the emission of radio frequencies. In his experiments with homeopathic potencies, a control solution showed no bio-information, while a D12 potency of platinum gave him peaks at 2.2 kHz and 4.5 kHz. Subsequently, I prepared a D12 potency of platinum and measured by dowsing the three frequencies: 2.301 kHz, 4.455 kHz, and 2.57 MHz. The last was obviously his radio frequency, and the others its modulation. I've detected similar resonances imprinted on water using light from an LED.

Elia and co-workers in Naples have carried out an extensive study on aqueous solutions subjected to successive dilutions and succussions. The heat of mixing with acids or bases differs between untreated water, dilute solutions, homeopathic potencies, and frequency-imprinted water. Although his microcalorimetry can confirm a single frequency imprint, it is at present too slow to measure a whole spectrum of frequencies.

IN THE FAR-INFRARED

When working toward a theory for "memory" effects in water, I looked at my measurements of the chemical hexane; this is a more volatile relative of the octane used for gasoline rating. With at least 14 ppm of water present, hexane gave a chemical frequency signature. Since it only has a spectrum in the far-infrared (FIR), this was the only region in which water could interact with it. Furthermore, I noted that of the very many water lines in this region, just a few [28 μm (357 cm^{-1}), 47 μm (213 cm^{-1}), and 78 μm (128 cm^{-1})] could become coherent enough to use in a water-vapor laser. I concluded that these should be able to provide the necessary coherence for water "memory" and was able to calculate hexane frequency signatures from these spectra.

When the same calculation was applied to pairs of these FIR lines in the absence of any hexane, this gave the measured frequencies of water. When a frequency was imprinted onto water, the FIR frequencies were replaced by two sidebands proportional to the imprinted frequency. Because of coherence, this is a *fractal* effect, and corresponding sidebands appeared in many parts of the electromagnetic spectrum.

A THEORETICAL BASIS FOR POTENTIZATION

When water was imprinted and then serially diluted, the original frequency disappeared, to be replaced by that frequency multiplied by the dilution ratio; but not all dilution ratios would do this. Some gave no frequencies. This provided a theoretical basis for the potentization of homeopathic remedies, which I demonstrated as follows. Water was imprinted with the complete pattern of frequencies previously determined for thyroxin of potency D15. This was further potentized by conventional serial dilutions and succussions. The frequencies measured for each synthesized potency were exactly the same as those for the potencies prepared from the "mother tincture" of thyroxin. Yet, my synthesized potencies had started from nothing but water. Importantly, there was no discontinuity at potency D24, which is the dilution at which not one molecule of the original substance should remain (Avogadro's number). This is where the chemists have to give up!

SHIELDING AND ERASURE

As already mentioned, it was during attempts to measure frequency imprints in water by instrumentation and in work with electrically hypersensitive patients and with homeopathic potencies that it was found that a potency or a water imprint would be erased if the geomagnetic field was shielded from it briefly with a steel box. Erasure must occur when the thermal energy is able to break up order due to magnetic energy. The water erasure threshold is about 1 percent of the Earth's magnetic field; the exact numbers imply a domain of phase coherence 53 µm in diameter. This threshold is independent of the imprinted frequency over at least the 13 decades from 10^{-4} Hz to 10^{+9} Hz. One microliter of water (acid or neutral) is needed to take up the imprint of a single frequency; but, if the water is alkaline, more is needed. The concentration of coherent domains in random water can be estimated from the number of imprints possible; the pH (acid/alkali) effect supports the involvement of protons.

In 1983, my laboratory showed that living systems can respond to magnetic resonance (NMR) conditions at geomagnetic field strengths. This high sensitivity allows one to speculate that a frequency might be retained in water if the magnetic resonance precession of the protons can be synchronized to any applied frequency and that they can generate an internal magnetic field that exactly satisfies the proton NMR conditions locally within their coherence domain. This condition turns out to be independent of the frequency to be remembered. Such a process would be stable unless a domain was thermally broken up by reducing the stabilizing geomagnetic field.

A 53 μm diameter domain contains more than enough protons to generate the magnetic field required to satisfy NMR conditions. The statistical fluctuation in the number of protons involved determines the bandwidth of the frequency imprint. This comes to about one part in a million (1 second at 1 MHz or 12 days at 1 Hz) and is consistent with the time needed for imprinting a frequency onto water by contact.

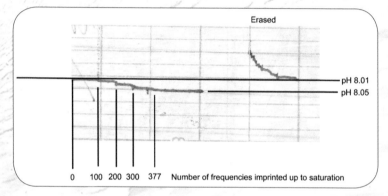

Change of pH on Frequency Imprinting: This chart recording shows that the pH of a solution of sodium hydroxide at pH 8.01 increased to pH 8.05 at memory saturation, which occurred after 377 separate imprinted frequencies. Erasure returned the pH to the initial value. An increase in pH corresponds to the removal of H+ ions and the generation of an equal number of OH- ions. The number of protons involved in this pH change for a single frequency imprint is sufficient to generate a local magnetic field to satisfy proton-NMR conditions independent of the imprinted frequency. Thus, imprinting a frequency into water may create a proton coherence that is sufficient to store that frequency. (Chart speed: 10min/div)

ICE PATTERNS

The ice patterns obtained by Dr. Masaru Emoto are reported to have been taken at magnifications of 100–200, where the microscope's field of view would be about 200–100 μm. They have a size and symmetry consistent with originating from a segment of the surface of a coherence domain about 50 μm diameter, the size I calculate from the water-memory erasure condition. These ice patterns are consistent with being a representation of frequency patterns within a domain. In 1989, we found that water frozen in a static magnetic field showed distinctive ice-crystal patterns directed at right angles to the magnetic field. There were also frequency-dependent effects from alternating magnetic fields. Therefore, ice-crystal patterns nucleated by coherent frequencies within a coherence domain remain at least a possibility.

CONCLUSION

Details relating to the contents of this chapter are to be found in the books I've listed in the Bibliography.

Finally, I'd like to recall the myth of Achilles and the tortoise, in which the choice of the wrong paradigm precluded the possibility of ever finding a solution to the point at which Achilles overtook the tortoise. For water, the appropriate paradigm is quantum physics. Ignore it, and make progress at tortoise speed.

◊ ◊ ◊

BIBLIOGRAPHY

C. W. Smith, "Electromagnetic Effects in Humans" in H. Fröhlich (ed.), *Biological Coherence and Response to External Stimuli,* Berlin: Springer-Verlag, 1988: pp.205–32.

——, "Coherent Electromagnetic Fields and Bio-Communication" in F-A. Popp, U. Warnke, H. L. König, W. Peschka (eds), *Electromagnetic Bio-Communication,* Munich, Baltimore: Urban & Schwarzenberg, 1989: pp.1–17.

C. W. Smith and S. Best, *Electromagnetic Man: Health and Hazard in the Electrical Environment.* London: Dent, 1989, 1990; New York: St. Martin's Press, 1989; Paris: Arys/Encre, 1995 (French edition), Bologna: Andromeda, 1997, 1998 (Italian editions).

C. W. Smith, "Electromagnetic and Magnetic Vector Potential Bio-Information and Water" in P. C. Endler, J. Schulte (eds), *Ultra High Dilution: Physiology and Physics,* Dordrecht: Kluwer Academic, 1994: pp.187–202.

——, "Effects of Electromagnetic Fields in the Living Environment; Proc. Intl. Conf. Electromagnetic Environments and Health in Buildings, Royal College of Physicians, London, 16–17 May, 2002" in D. Clements-Croome (ed.), *Electromagnetic Environments and Health in Buildings,* London: Taylor & Francis, October 2003: Chap. 3, pp.53–118.

——, "Fröhlich's Interpretation of Biology through Theoretical Physics" in G. J. Hyland and P. Rowlands (eds), *Herbert Fröhlich FRS: A Physicist Ahead of his Time,* Liverpool: University of Liverpool, 2006: pp.91–138.

WEBSITES

American Environmental Health Foundation, Dallas:
www.aehf.com

Breakspear Hospital, Hemel Hempstead, UK:
www.break spearmedical.com

Newsletter by Simon Best (co-author of *Electromagnetic Man*):
www.em-hazard-therapy.com

CHAPTER 4

WATER: NATURE'S MIRACLE—
BEYOND SCIENTIFIC EXPLANATION

by Dolly Knight and Jonathan Stromberg

Apart from the many well-researched properties of water, which make it unique as the life supporter of this planet, there is one ability of water that mainstream science has tried to ignore and deny: the "memory of water" phenomenon. This phenomenon lies beyond the accepted level of scientific inquiry, and little effort has been made by conventional research institutes to understand it. However there are exceptions, and an exciting new understanding of the marvelous properties of water is emerging.

VIBRATIONAL IMPRINTING

Various researchers, such as Professor Jacques Benveniste, Dr. Wolfgang Ludwig, David Schweitzer, and Masaru Emoto, have provided clear proof that water acts as a liquid tape recorder and is able to receive, store, and transmit electromagnetic vibrations. Because water molecules have a positive and negative pole, they behave like little magnets. They attach themselves to their neighboring molecules and form clusters of several hundred molecules. These clusters are very sensitive structures and are impressionable by vibrational influences. This is what gives water the ability to store information.

This is closely linked to homeopathy, where a substance is diluted so many times that eventually there's virtually no molecule of the original substance left, yet it still has an effect. Homeopathy works because of the cluster ability to store vibrational imprints. Every substance and element has its own individual vibrational pattern, a bit like an energy blueprint. If one carries out the homeopathic process of diluting and succussing, the vibrational pattern of the remedy material becomes locked into the cluster structure of the carrier water. When you take this homeopathically prepared remedy, the cluster structure is transferred to the body, and you react to the vibrational pattern of the original substance from which the remedy was prepared.

This phenomenon was shown to occur under rigid scientific conditions by Jacques Benveniste in France in the late 1980s and was confirmed by researchers at five different universities. It caused quite a stir and subsequently a cover-up by the mainstream scientific community.

If water is this susceptible to vibrational imprinting, does it also take on the imprints of environmental pollutants and chemicals with which it has been in contact, and transfer them to us when we drink it?

Unfortunately, this seems to be the case. In Germany, Wolfgang Ludwig has carried out tests that show that not only does the *physical* pollutant have a damaging effect, but so does the *water* that has been exposed to the pollutant, because the cluster structure has taken on the vibrational imprint of the pollutant.

This has huge ramifications for us. Basically, conventional water and sewage treatment systems are not adequate. They may remove the *physical* pollutants and produce tap water that's chemically clean. However, the cluster structure of the water is completely unaffected by the treatment and will still convey the vibrational pattern of toxins and chemicals to the human body.

IMPLOSION

However, all is not lost, thanks to the intriguing work of the Austrian forester Viktor Schauberger (1885–1958). He had ample opportunity to study the workings of nature in unspoiled Alpine forests. Being an extremely intuitive man, very much in tune with the natural world, he soon developed ideas and theories regarding nature, and particularly water, that were in conflict with conventional scientific understanding. Early on, he discovered that there was an underlying principle governing all natural processes. He called this "implosion."

Schauberger became a prolific writer and inventor. His inventions were linked to water supply, natural river regulation, agriculture, propulsion, and energy generation, and were all based on implosion. He's very important to us in that he pointed out a new way of looking at nature and exciting new possibilities—if nature's true workings could be really understood and copied in a technological sense.

Implosion is a suctional process that causes matter to move inward, not outward, as in the case of explosion. This inward (centripetal) motion doesn't, however, follow a straight (radial) path to the center, but a spiraling, whirling path. This is called a *vortex* and is the secret of nature. Bathwater, when emptied, flows through the plug hole in this spiraling vortex fashion. Water will always try to follow the path of least resistance. This is what the vortex is enabling it to do. It's reducing resistance by curving inward more and more, thereby avoiding the confrontational resistance of straight motion.

The vortex motion, which also causes a drop in temperature and increase in density, is paramount for water to stay healthy and disease free. Natural water courses are naturally spiraling and meandering, and the water in them forms whirls and eddies, which are vortices. In nature there are virtually no straight forms; and whenever possible, vortices, spirals, and curves are produced to reduce resistance. Yet in conventional technology, explosion, combustion, and straight motion are employed, all of which increase resistance and temperature and are fundamentally against nature. Realization of this caused Schauberger to proclaim emphatically: "Our technologists are moving matter incorrectly. Their technologies and interference with nature are detrimental to us and our planet."

RE-ENERGIZING WATER

After researching Viktor Schauberger for a couple of years, we were convinced that he had something very important to impart to humanity. Sadly, not a lot of work has been carried out in the last few decades on developing practical applications for his ideas. So we started full-time research in September 1997 and developed an implosion machine. In this machine, water is made to form very powerful vortices. We found that water undergoing this process of implosion was developing a rhythmically pulsating field of energy, which comprised the full spectrum of etheric colors. During this process, it was brought back to its natural vibrant energetic state and regained its life force. This energetic charge turned out to be permanent and didn't diminish after the implosion process was completed.

We further discovered that when filled into particular shapes, this imploded water transferred its energy to samples of ordinary non-energized water until they reached the same level of charge as the imploded water. The imploded water was resonating ordinary water in a similar fashion to the way one tuning fork picks up the vibrations of another, the difference being that on the etheric level, the vortical dynamics and vibrations are perpetual.

After building the implosion machine, we developed a spiraling copper device called the "Vortex Energiser," in which we filled our imploded water. We found that placing this Vortex Energiser onto the domestic water mains resonated the tap water flowing past, thereby charging it up with life force or etheric energy. The benefits of energizing ordinary tap water in this way are varied: The clarity and taste of the water improve—the water is more palatable and less hard; the taste and smell of chlorine are much reduced or even eliminated; lime-scale deposits become soft and are eventually removed; bathing in energized water is a reviving experience, leaving skin supple and soft; fresh food and cut flowers washed with or placed in the water last longer.

Perhaps most important, by reclustering water and at the same time energizing it in this way, we believe that we're superimposing a natural vibrational pattern onto a pattern of man-made contaminants, thereby deleting the memory of the water's abused past.

○ ○ ○

REFERENCES AND FURTHER READING

O. Alexandersson, *Living Water: Viktor Schauberger and the Secrets of Natural Energy,* Bath, UK: Gateway Books, 1996.

T. Batmanghelidj, *Your Body's Many Cries for Water,* Worthing, UK: The Therapist Ltd, 1997.

S. Best and D. W. Smith, *Electromagnetic Man: Health and Hazard in the Electrical Environment,* London: J. M. Dent & Sons Ltd, 1989.

P. S. Callahan, *Paramagnetism: Rediscovering Nature's Secret Force of Growth,* Austin, TX: Acres USA, 1995.

——, *Exploring the Spectrum: Wavelengths of Agriculture and Life,* Austin, TX: Acres USA, 1995.

C. Coats, *Living Energies: Viktor Schauberger's Brilliant Work with Natural Energy Explained,* Bath, UK: Gateway Books, 1996.

R. Coghill, *Something in the Air,* Lower Race, Pontypool, Wales, NP4 5UH, UK: Self-published, 1997.

A. Hall, *Water, Electricity and Health,* Stroud, UK: Hawthorn Press, 1997.

W. Ludwig, in *Umweltmedizin,* eds Treven and Talkenhammer, Idstein, Germany: Mowe-Verlag, 1991.

F. A. Popp, 1979, in *Bioresonance and Multiresonance Therapy,* ed. Brugemann, Hans Haug International, vol. I., 1993.

M. Schiff, *The Memory of Water: Homoeopathy and the Battle of Ideas in the New Science,* London: HarperCollins, 1995; also published in German by Zweitausendeins.

THE CENTRE FOR IMPLOSION RESEARCH

The CIR was founded in December 1997 by Dolly Knight, MBBS, GCHM, and Jonathan Stromberg, BSc, MSc, DIC, FGS. We believe everyone has a duty to do whatever they can to improve our ailing planet's environmental condition. Our aim is to develop technologies that are simple and pollution free and work in harmony with nature.

For further information please contact:

The Centre for Implosion Research, PO Box 38,
Plymouth, PL7 5YX, UK
Tel: (44) 1752 345552; Fax: (44) 1752 338569
E-mail: **info@implosionresearch.com**
Website: **www.implosionresearch.com**

○○○ ○○○

CHAPTER 5

SNOW, IT HAS SIX EDGES

by Maximilian Glas

It was deep in the winter of 1611 when the mathematician and astronomer Johannes Kepler crossed over a bridge in Frankfurt and fine snowflakes drifted down onto him, "all in the form of the hexagon with feathered rays," he wrote. "It is always like this when it starts to snow—snowflakes always form hexagonal stars—and there must be a definite reason for it. If it happens by chance, why don't they form heptagons or pentagons. . . .?"[1]

Around 400 years ago, nobody knew how matter was constructed, how crystals grew, or what inner laws the formation of crystals followed. Kepler was the first person in the modern age to seriously think about the subject and to develop a coherent model. It would be another 300 years before the Munich physicist Max von Laue proved this model correct. Fortunately for us, Kepler wrote down his reflections in 1611. He not only handed down a pioneering thought, but one that made it easy to understand why all snow crystals (and respectively ice or water crystals) form symmetries based on the number 6, and this leads us to the fascinating pictures from Masaru Emoto.

Kepler dedicated his Latin script *De nive sexangula* (About the hexagonal snow) to Counsellor Knight Wackher von Wackenfels, a well-known philosopher, as a "New Year's gift." He wanted to delight the enthusiastic nihilist with a present that came as close as possible to "nothingness": just a little star formed out of snow, along with a few thoughts about it. In these thoughts,

Kepler pondered on how the little star could have grown and concluded that it would have very slowly condensed out of the steam in the air.

THE MEANING OF FORM

Kepler's thoughts regarding form were: "Only that which forms a boundary in itself has a form, because the boundaries shape the forms."

That is clear, but why a hexagon of all forms? Kepler continued:

> It needed further consideration as to what was at work here. Was the form innate or produced from the outside? Was the hexagonal figure necessitated by the material out of which it was formed, or by its own nature, which was either the prototype of beauty which lies in a hexagon or due to the aim of this figure.[2]

So, inner or outer necessity—a clear, beautiful train of thought!

After this, Kepler developed the concept of the construction of "solid bodies" from minute units, which ideally should possess a spherical form. That means that he had the first vision of what's today called an atom. He also had an understanding of the order of the spheres. He assumed that the order was level, and there were layers over layers, which is what formed the crystal. This is still the current view. He concluded that at least two possibilities existed: that the order of the spheres formed a square (A) or a triangle (B). He even illustrated this:

In a second sketch, he showed the spatial construction: Layer A (with a sphere) is placed on layer B, and this then on C, and so on. Finally, a pyramid is formed by four equilateral triangles—therefore a tetrahedron—which shows threefold symmetry, and

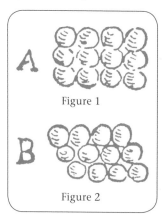

Figure 1

Figure 2

that has to be the architectural basis for constructing "snow stars."

Obviously, Kepler didn't know the construction of water molecules at that point and so wasn't able to foresee the necessity of the sixfold (not threefold) symmetry, but in any event it can be derived from the threefold symmetry.

All in all, this was a stroke of genius! Kepler had described the construction of snow crystals in nearly the same way that it would be today. And all this 400 years ago, without the model of an atom, without developed crystallography, and without the help of technical instruments. Crystals are still described today as a three-dimensional spatial grid made up of spherical particles (atoms). And, as mentioned at the beginning, Max von Laue was able to confirm the structure of crystals through x-ray experiments in 1912.

In the case of water, the crystal structure is determined by the shape and form of the H_2O molecule. Contrary to what Kepler expected, the spherical density is less than he showed in his second sketch, but is formed of a looser group of molecules, which are ordered as a tetrahedron and combine to form little rings of six:

The sketch shows a small section of the crystal structure of ice and puts it in the context of the hexagon. It also explains why ice has a bigger volume than water and consequently is lighter and able to float on water: As ice, there's relatively a lot of space between the individual components; in the fluid state, water is denser. Around

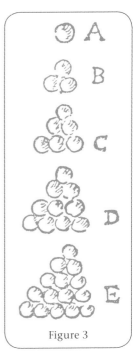

Figure 3

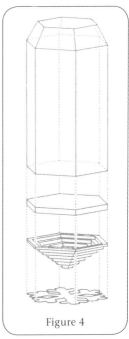

Figure 4

two to four million water molecules of this structure are needed to be able to build around 0.039 inches (1 millimeter) of one edge of an ice crystal. The connection of the H_2O molecules in the crystal grid is made through hydrogen bridges, which also play an important role in the formation of clusters.

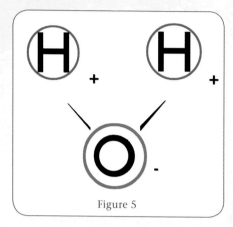

Figure 5

IT BEGINS WITH A SEED

As easy as it might seem to understand the inner structure of ice crystals, in the living process of growth many different things can occur; and those change and shape the outer form of the finished crystals. Ice crystals can look completely different depending on what happened during the growth process.

At first this starts very simply. As Kepler discovered in 1611 on the bridge in Frankfurt, water begins to condense at some point. That means that steam forms fine droplets, which slowly crystallize and harden in low temperatures according to the "construction plan" already described.

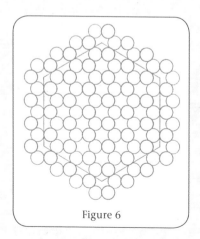

Figure 6

In order for a crystal to be able to form, a "seed" is needed: a tiny unit of the grid on which the water molecules can settle, layer upon layer. Such a seed can come from pure water, which in low enough temperatures develops spontaneously into a droplet and afterward into a crystal seed with a regular internal construction. But fine floating dust particles in the air can also trigger the formation of an ordered crystal structure.

Once such a seed has been formed, there's nothing to stop it from growing. Layer upon layer of water molecules settle on it in all directions—but not in all directions to the same degree. Depending on pressure and the temperature of the atmosphere, this can be very different. If the process is taking place at great heights and in low temperatures, most of the crystals assume an elongated form, often appearing as very long, fine ice needles, but always with a hexagonal cross section. On the sketch (see Figure 4), this is the top part. The upper end of the crystal is able to develop even more surface area.

More is shown in this sketch. If the conditions aren't very icy, but there's still thick frost, six mainly flat lateral slabs will develop; below, one can see an ice-crystal cup, a form that can be seen in the ice caves of the Alps (sometimes at enormous heights). The last form is a snowflake as we all know it. These are just the simple basic forms—what nature creates out of these is unique.

ENORMOUS FREEDOM OF CREATIVITY

Every single ice crystal is unique. Even with millions of crystals, no two will be identical. A pair might look like identical twins, but they'll never be exactly the same. This is because every single one comes from heaven to Earth in its very own way. On their journey, these crystals pass through different layers of air, each with different pressure, temperature, humidity, and pollution; and the falling snowflakes react to every small change.

Let's consider how a clean crystallized hexagonal ice-slab leaves the clouds and starts its journey down to Earth. If it passes through a warmer layer of air, the edge of the slab will get loose; if it goes through a colder layer, new crystal layers may be taken up. Sometimes this can happen quickly, sometimes slowly; sometimes the growth phases are long, sometimes extremely short; sometimes there's more humidity in the air, sometimes less.

We all know from experience how different these crystals can turn out to be. In the never-ending process of growth and dissolution, the most bizarre shapes can form. Everything is possible.

If at one point it gets too warm, the crystals will dissolve completely before reaching Earth, and it will start to rain. Sometimes the droplets will cross layers of ice and become fine hailstones, and so on. There are no limits to nature's imagination.

This variety has always been a source of fascination and several people have tried to "collect" these ice crystals. This is much harder than with other minerals, due to the temperatures involved, although it's just possible with the help of photography. The craziest collection belonged to the American W. A. Bentley. He built himself a special slab-camera and spent winter after winter on a mountain in Vermont, taking pictures of thousands of snow crystals. In 1931 a book of 2,453 of his ice-crystal pictures was published.[3] A selection of these follows.

Snow-crystals photographed by W.A. Bentley.

So much for the rather conventional scientific descriptions of the development of ice crystals. These are always related to pressure, temperature, and other outer conditions. Masaru Emoto's research has introduced a new aspect, a mental and spiritual one, as he has shown that the subtle energies and vibrations of thoughts, words, and sounds obviously have an impact on the growth of crystals— quite a radical thought for the more orthodox mineralogist. The path of progress here, as in science generally, has been toward investigating ever-smaller sizes and ever-finer energies. It would be wrong to think that this path isn't being blocked by outdated dogma. But maybe these ice crystals will inspire us, as they did Kepler 400 years ago, to revise our concept of the world.

○ ○ ○

NOTES

1. Johannes Kepler, *De nive sexangula,* 1611: p. 92.

2. Ibid.

3. W. A. Bentley and W. J. Humphreys, *Snow Crystals,* New York: Dover Publications, 1931, reprinted 1962.

○○○ ○○○

PART II

HEALTH AND
HEALING PERSPECTIVES

INTRODUCTION

The scientific section of this book described the remarkable properties of water as discovered by scientists in recent years. This portion takes these discoveries and builds on them, showing how we can use water in many ways to maintain our health and fight disease. It will be seen that water does this in two interconnected ways: through its well-known physical properties, and through its more hidden spiritual qualities.

The human body is composed of around 85 percent water, which performs many life-sustaining tasks. For example, it supports complex biochemical reactions, provides structural support for cells, and is the major component in blood and all other body fluids. Also very important, it eliminates dangerous waste products from every part of the organism. These processes all rely on water's physical properties. From my own and other scientists' work with water and water crystals, I'm convinced that there's a profound interaction between our thoughts (and perhaps those of people around us) and the water in our bodies. Positive thoughts affect the molecular structure of bodily water, and thus the health and well-being of the entire organism. This theme is central to all the papers in this section. They advance original and important insights into the value of water for healing, and have all been written by experienced health practitioners who have been pioneers of new ideas and information.

An important paper here is on dowsing—the use of divination to find water. This ancient technique, still in constant use around the world, demonstrates yet more of the astonishing powers of water—in particular, the ability to make itself felt from a distance, and from under many layers of rock.

I hope that you'll make use of the ideas and suggestions in these papers for your own well-being and for that of your friends, family, and communities.

○○○ ○○○

CHAPTER 6

WATER AS A SOURCE OF HEALTH

by Petra Bracht, M.D.

Water is essential to our well-being, but its powerful beneficial effect on our health can all too often go unacknowledged. Because all metabolic processes need fluids, it's of huge importance that the "primeval sea" in which the cells swim is always in sufficient supply. To get a better understanding of the crucial role water plays in our health, it's important to consider the physiological processes behind illness and well-being.

WHAT MAKES PEOPLE ILL?

Most people think that illness comes from outside and out of the blue, almost as if an enemy is there lying in wait for the right opportunity to launch an attack. In the Middle Ages, evil ghosts and demons were blamed. Today these have been replaced by fungi, viruses, and bacteria. Contrary to orthodox medical belief, however, each illness has its origin in our psyche; hence, its nature isn't material. What manifests at the physical level (that is, the symptoms) is the body's effort to fight illness; and it's at this level that we can positively influence the "dis-ease" process, as the physical self has infinite potential to secure the support of its 80 billion cells.

All simple illnesses can be seen as the body's attempt to dispose of "rubbish" (for example, through a cold or skin impurities) or to kill undesired substances through increasing the body temperature. It's only if the body has been abused for many years or if extremely toxic substances have made their way into it that this maintenance mechanism breaks down. Then we start having problems with our health and illness breaks out, and in time it might become chronic.

Although germs are present all the time in the body, they very rarely trigger noticeable symptoms if there's a healthy immune system. This process is similar to cancer in that in nearly every human body cancer cells arise repeatedly on a daily basis. Yet some people get cancer, while others don't. Why is this? Here too the immune system plays a decisive role. So the question is, how can we strengthen our immune system?

First of all, if our metabolism is functioning properly, it will guarantee optimal support for all our cells. An optimal metabolism also means optimal elimination of waste material and harmful substances. But how can we exert a positive influence on our metabolism? What can we do to ensure it helps maintain us in the best of health?

MEGALOPOLIS, THE CITY OF THE BODY

Can you imagine a crowd of 80 billion people? A megalopolis, a concentration of several big cities into one megacity? Probably not. There are some six billion people alive on our planet today, but nearly 80 billion cells in the body are in communication with each other every single second. A protective wall—the skin—encloses our city, where "people"—cells—of all kinds live together. Food and other materials are mainly brought in from outside, although some food is produced within the protective wall by the body's own chemical factory.

Transport within the city is provided by water. The main part of the incoming material is delivered by a river that runs through the city, then this cargo is unloaded and distributed. The waste material is loaded onto ships farther down the river, which leave the city with the current. A very clever distribution system within the city ensures that everything arrives where it's needed.

An equally well-thought-out disposal system carries everything that's no longer needed outside so that there's no accumulation of toxic waste.

So how, in such an organized city, can people still die of starvation, buildings collapse, or stinky wastelands (germ beds) develop and threaten a whole quarter? The answer is very simple: If you supply this city with inferior building materials or block its main transport routes, you basically turn off its water supply. However, as long as the city is provided with everything that it needs and enough water is available, everything will work smoothly.

Each person is such a perfectly functioning city. We all have the best infrastructure that anyone could ever design. None of the most modern supercomputers can match it, but far too few people are aware that it's only through the continued supply of good-quality water that all these processes run smoothly.

INNER MOVEMENT

Everything, even the smallest process inside us, is based on movement. That's why we function best when in motion. This is true for our immune system, the inner organs, the cardiovascular system, the musculoskeletal system, the nerves, the lymphatic system, the brain, and the emotions. We can influence a whole range of metabolic processes through movement. Let's have a closer look at what happens during these metabolic processes.

The raw materials and tools that the body needs to function properly are carbohydrates, fat, protein, vitamins and enzymes, trace elements, minerals, and fiber. These have to be taken in and transported to the part of the body where a specific process happens. At this "building site," new cells are constructed, as are hormones, enzymes, protein, certain vitamins, and much more. All these are produced in the body's own laboratories. Old cells, meanwhile, die off and are recycled. Waste material is produced, which is discharged with the help of special detoxification organs (kidneys, intestines, skin, and lungs). Now you start to get an idea of how much is going on in your body every second of your life.

The means of transport that makes all this possible is water. Our body has a very complex network of "pipes"—blood vessels—so that every cell can be supplied with the necessary materials. Obviously, the efficiency of the system depends on the condition of the network. Many factors have an impact on the smooth running of the organization, but there's one that's fundamental: movement. This is the primary secret of life.

Movement is life; stagnation is death! The driving force behind all movement is our muscular system. The muscles ensure that blood, lymph, and all other bodily fluids are transported throughout the body and support the work of the heart. Moving the body is therefore beneficial for the heart. Movement stimulates circulation; and as a result our pipes are "flushed out," all the cells are supplied with oxygen, all the nutrients reach their "place of work," the detoxification organs run at top speed, and all the necessary hormones and enzymes are produced.

When everything is moving along so well, something phenomenal happens: Our body starts to notice that the pipes could actually be bigger and that more pipes would ensure an even better supply, or perhaps that certain areas have not been supplied at all. The body gives immediate instructions to begin the necessary building work. The existing vessels get bigger, new ones are added, and the network is extended. The bones get stronger, and the cartilage and vertebrae get thicker so that they're able to take the additional strain. The organs are refurbished so that they can work more efficiently. The improved supply also explains why the bones of a person who does physical exercise heal more quickly than those of someone who doesn't. Just to give you an idea of the scale of the process, muscles that move have a circulation rate 200 times higher than those that remain at rest. This means that those cells will be 200 times better supplied with building materials and oxygen, and waste will be discharged 200 times faster.

It's hard to imagine, but if all the body's blood vessels were laid end to end, they would be about 60,000 miles in length and would circle the Earth more than twice. These vessels are our body's highways.

We could look around the "building site" of our body for hours and find endless new adjustments being made, all triggered by our movements. These can only take place, however, if there is enough water, in the form of blood, to flush through the 60,000 miles of blood vessels.

Movement in our body is better described as "perpetual motion." Once it has started, the system responds by moving more and more. If it's activated every day, this will trigger a dance of joy in the body. Outer activity will also bring about easier inner movement. If there's no movement, the heart will simply maintain its most basic rate—sadly, a condition that most people live with today, without even knowing it. The system that's most affected in this case is the body's oxygen supply. If you don't lead an active life, your body is just getting an emergency supply, and your cells are "gasping for breath." Many important illnesses—such as circulation problems, headaches, impotence, and insomnia—arise through a poor supply of oxygen. And for a proper amount, you need water.

A HUMAN BEING IS A WATER BEING

Movement, satisfaction, and good food are the main prerequisites for health, which goes hand in hand with beauty. Natural, healthy beauty starts inside the body. If everything is in good order on the inside, it will be on the outside, too. Your skin will be healthy, because there will be no need for waste products to be brought to the surface for elimination. Therefore, the condition of the skin, the outer loveliness, mirrors the inner beauty. If your body contains enough water, for example, your skin will be smooth and elastic and your eyes bright. Your body will be functioning at its optimal level. The water content in babies is often as much as 75 percent, but this will continually decrease with age. Unfortunately, it's not unusual to find levels of under 50 percent in adults. Even young people show low levels of water.

WATER AS TRANSPORT

Water is the main means of transport not only for all the materials that are required by the cells, but also for all the cells' waste substances. If the transport network isn't functioning properly because of a lack of water, waste isn't taken away, but left behind. In medical terminology, this is a "deposit." Physicians talk, for example, about the uric acid crystals that trigger a gout attack, and a person is described as "calcified" when part of their brain has become a salt deposit. Deposits may also collect in the blood vessels over a period of time until one day they trigger a heart attack, stroke, or lung embolism.

HOW AND WHAT SHOULD YOU DRINK?

Many people think that they have done their duty by drinking four pints of water per day. But only a few individuals manage to accomplish this; and those who do drink the recommended amount of water often do so in a way that's very ineffective, because pouring several pints of water into the body, say, twice a day, once in the morning and once in the evening, isn't a very sensible thing to do. Such a large amount can't be used properly and will just pass through the body. It's far more sensible to drink water throughout the day. This then has enough time to trickle through the blood vessels into the spaces between the cells and from there into the cells themselves.

The water we drink should be as soft as possible. Nobody would expect their washing machine to use hard, calcified water. Just as soft water is more effective for washing clothes because it can penetrate more deeply into the fabric, so it's more effective for our body, as it can reach even the most remote corners. Therefore, you should drink still, soft water with only traces of calcium and minerals.

This is contrary to current opinion, which recommends exactly the opposite. Ads for "healing" waters particularly emphasize the high concentration and number of different minerals they contain. The culmination of this is fitness drinks with a high mix of minerals. However, more and more therapists now agree that too much of a good thing can have a negative effect. They share the opinion that minerals that haven't been taken in through the biological bond can't be used to optimal effect, which means they're actually not available to the cells. On the contrary, it's often impossible for the body to dispose of these surpluses, and so they accumulate in the space between the cells. In the longer term, this may result in a system overload and the metabolic processes becoming dangerously restricted.

PURE WATER FOR A LONG LIFE

There's an old Chinese phrase that's often found in ancient texts: "water of long life." This kind of water was collected, with immense effort, from the high mountain region and was only available to the upper classes. It was either rainwater or "dew-water" from melted snow. It was pure, having been cleansed naturally through evaporation or rainfall. Unfortunately, this process can no longer take place—today there are many particles in the atmosphere that pollute rainwater.

According to traditional Chinese wisdom, the health benefits of pure water were far-reaching. Although this belief is easy

Above: Fresh spring water that originates at the bottom of a mountain. A shining vibrant crystal has formed, which expresses the original power and beauty of nature.

to understand from a biophysical point of view, it meets with resistance from conventional medicine.

Two arguments are often put forward against the consumption of pure water. The first is osmotic pressure. This is demonstrated by putting animal cells into pure water in a reagent glass. The cells blow up till they finally burst, because fluids with different part concentrations have the tendency to reach the same concentration. So more and more water goes into the cells until the cell wall isn't able to cope with the growing pressure and bursts. The opponents of the pure-water theory assume that the same would actually happen in the human body. This is of course a mistake, as the conditions aren't the same. Water begins its journey in the mouth; and right from the start, it's no longer pure. Furthermore, the deeper it goes into the body, the more polluted it becomes. This cleansing effect is what gives the result the Chinese describe: a longer life.

The second argument against the consumption of pure water is that it washes precious minerals out of the body, causing a deficiency. Earlier on, however, we saw how water with a strong mineral or calcium content created deposits in between the cells, hindering the metabolism. Flushing these deposits out of the body is exactly why we need to drink pure water. Furthermore, the body measures precisely the levels of minerals it discharges—it doesn't give up those that it needs. If necessary, it will go so far as to take back through the skin minerals that have been dispersed through perspiration. (This was discovered by Japanese scientists who were examining athletes.) This means that the argument against drinking pure water is actually the very reason why it's beneficial for health.

If only it wasn't serious, this might even be funny—in the U.S. and in many Asian countries, pure or distilled water is on sale in supermarkets, and in Thailand it's even marketed with the slogan: "This water is good for your health!" At the same time, in Germany and other European countries, medical students learn that it can be dangerous, perhaps even life-threatening.

In my own family, we've drunk pure water for more than ten years for the good of our health; my husband consumes nearly six pints a day. He's in good health and very fit. By the way, did you know that coffee and tea made out of distilled water taste much better, and that it also makes good beer and baby food?

WHERE CAN I GET PURE WATER?

If you live in a country where you can't buy pure water, then you can make it yourself. To do this, you can either filter or distill water through evaporation. In fact, evaporation is the way nature itself cleanses water. The only difference is that in nature it's cold distillation, and at home it's hot distillation.

In the hot-distillation process, water is heated to the point of evaporation and then spirals its way back down into liquid form. The impurities are left behind in the container in which the water has been heated. This is actually a good test for your tap water. Fill a big cooking pan from your faucet, and let it evaporate. Afterward, have a look at the residue in the bottom of your pan. If you live in a congested area or somewhere with very hard water, this experience should be enough to make you start drinking pure water immediately!

In the steam-distillation process, the order of hydrogen and oxygen molecules in the water is changed, and as a result it can lose its beneficial "information." To counteract this, it's a good idea to put the distilled water out in the sun, shake it, stir it, or even play it pleasant music. In this way you load it with positive intent.

The alternative is filtering. There are many ways to do this, but all of them have the same problem as vacuum cleaners: On one hand, the filter must be fine enough so that no dirt can get through, but on the other hand it must be coarse enough so that it doesn't get blocked by the dirt it picks up. A lot of the filter systems on the market claim to have struck such a balance, but who knows what, if any, minerals are getting through? And water without any minerals at all would be what they call "dead water"—that's why the filters on our taps don't remove all the minerals.

What are the criteria for "living" water anyway? Is water from fruit alive? Is fresh spring water alive, because it forms beautiful crystals? We can certainly say that it isn't the existence of minerals that determines the vitality of water, but the information that's contained in the water. And this can't be viewed on the material level alone. We should consider the etheric energy of water here, not just the way impurities and minerals are filtered out of it.

Those who want to purify water thoroughly, however, can do this through the reverse-osmosis procedure. Here water runs through a very fine filter membrane. The pores of this are so small that the purity of the water is as good as when it's distilled. Reverse-osmosis filters can be connected to the main pipes from under the kitchen sink. Then, to revitalize your distilled water, you can use one of the methods described earlier.

EATING WATER IS BETTER THAN DRINKING IT

The best possible way for the body to get water is out of fruits and vegetables. In this way, all minerals, trace elements, and vitamins are easily available, as well as all the other plant substances that have benefited humankind for millions of years.

Water that's consumed in this manner reaches the blood more slowly and evenly and at the same time that the minerals are offered in the biological bond. Therefore, the body is able to use both water and minerals much more effectively. Thus, the best way to provide your body with water is to eat it.

Above: Distilled water that has been shown the movie *Life*.
The water seems animated and formed a beautiful crystal.

It's not difficult to do. The water content of most fruit and vegetables is over 90 percent. For melons, oranges, and grapes, it's as high as 98 percent. Therefore, "eat" water whenever you can—that way, "drinking" becomes a real pleasure. A fruit salad or an apple makes a delicious snack and helps you stay healthy as well.

Cooking and frying dehydrate food, so the best way to eat fruits and vegetables is as fresh as possible. Fish and meat also lose water when cooked; and the higher the temperature, the greater the water loss. That's why we should try to cook our food at the lowest temperature possible. This has also the advantage of improving the taste.

AND DON'T FORGET—DRINK A LOT!

If for the last decade you've been drinking far too little water, or have drunk it in such a way that your body hasn't been able to use it properly, the consequences will become more and more apparent in the second half of your life. The very sad fact that older people often don't cook for themselves anymore and tend to rely on ready-made meals, which often have minimal water content, also contributes to the water shortage they experience.

So why not turn this around and make a positive change? The older you get, the more water you should drink and the more fresh food you should eat. This will help keep you physically and mentally agile well into old age.

Above: Eat fruits that are as fresh as possible.

COLONIC IRRIGATION: CLEANSING AND DETOXING WITH WATER

Thousands of years ago, enemas were used to enhance the healing process. Today the same process is used, but with a completely different technique. Colonic hydrotherapy, which was developed for U.S. astronauts, is able to clean the colon thoroughly and hygienically. The flush effect enables the removal of all the old decaying material—fecal matter—which can lead to recurrent poisoning. Through the osmotic process, it's also possible to reach and remove toxic substances beyond the colon quickly and easily, without any side effects. This process can have dramatic results—in some cases, hay fever and migraines have disappeared completely after just one treatment. Former smokers also experience fewer withdrawal symptoms.

The colon has a huge (approximately 3,230 square foot) interface with the interior of the body. With colonic irrigation, metabolic residues and toxic waste matter can be taken up by the water that has been introduced into the colon, and thus eventually leave the body through the rectum. If your lifestyle needs to be healthier, having this "internal shower" once or twice a year will give you a much-needed opportunity to cleanse yourself of metabolic residues and enable you to experience the healing power of water.

CHAPTER 7

WATER: THE FUSION OF SCIENCE AND SPIRIT

by Dr. Darren R. Weissman

Conscious living, I've learned, begins with understanding the true power of water, as documented through the research of Dr. Masaru Emoto. The power of water exists in its ability to flow effortlessly, no matter what its environment. Water takes on the shape of its container, moves continually in swirling motions, or is effortlessly guided by the banks of a river. As life itself, it's always moving, changing from one state to another, vibrating and resonating at different frequencies. It has the potential to carve a path through a mountain, squeeze through the smallest opening, and, when heated, evaporate into thin air. Water is as mysterious as the infinite universe itself. It holds the secrets of all life. One drop may contain the blueprint for the cure of every disease known to humankind.

The human body is estimated to be between 70 and 90 percent water. Each cell, organ, and system of the body consists of specific percentages of water; and the flow of that water determines whether the body expresses itself in optimal health or in symptoms of imbalance or disease.

The late F. Batmanghelidj, M.D., a renowned physician, researcher, and author of *Your Body's Many Cries for Water*, discovered the profound benefits water has on the physiological functions of the body. He wrote:

From the new perspective of my 22 years of clinical and scientific research into molecular physiology of dehydration . . . I can safely say the 60 million Americans with hypertension, the 110 million with chronic pains, the 15 million with diabetes, the 17 million with asthma, and the 50 million with allergies . . . all waited to get thirsty. Had they realized water [was] a natural antihistamine and a more effective diuretic, these people would have been saved the agony of their health problems.

This article will outline the healing power of water and how the subsequent fusion of science and spirit gave birth to The LifeLine Technique.

DR. EMOTO'S WORK AS A CATALYST

It was the groundbreaking water-crystal research of Dr. Emoto that demonstrated the essence of water's power—its *consciousness*—and the instantaneous impact our thoughts, words, and actions have on its molecular structure. Because every element, cell, organ, and system of the human body is composed of water, we now understand that emotions affect the health of the body in the same way that the water in the crystal research was affected.

Dr. Emoto's work was the catalyst for The LifeLine Technique, which makes it possible for us to *understand* what the body is *saying* when it speaks to us in symptoms. Incorporating aspects of 14 natural healing modalities, The LifeLine Technique is based on the ancient arts of Chinese and Ayurvedic medicines, as well as on years of empiricism, documented research, and biomedical evidence. Through the use of a kinesiological reflex (muscle test), a LifeLine practitioner is able to translate, harmonize, and facilitate the release of emotions trapped within the subconscious mind, thereby enabling the body to heal on a core level. Coupled with healthy lifestyle choices—such as the quantity, quality, and frequency of water, food, rest, and exercise and owning your power—The LifeLine Technique awakens people to the power of living consciously.

My journey to awakening to The LifeLine Technique was the culmination of every experience, teacher, and patient with whom I worked. Each modality I learned and used provided another piece of the puzzle I was constructing in an effort to find the link that would ultimately help my patients heal at the deepest of levels. When it all finally came together, the missing link turned out to be Dr. Emoto. His discovery of the secret life of water forever changed my view of the body's healing potential.

I want to share a portion of my journey with you. During the summer of 1998, my cousin Rob Morgan worked as an intern in my office in preparation for becoming the first deaf chiropractor ever to graduate from the Palmer College of Chiropractic. After a full day of observing patients, Rob turned to me and held up his hand in what I was to learn meant "I love you" in sign language.

"I love you"

I was amazed by the warm, powerful, and peaceful feeling I experienced as Rob held up his hand. Intrigued by this sensation, I asked him to hold his arm up as I assessed different reflex points on his body using a muscle test. (A muscle test uses an indicator muscle or involuntary reflex to evaluate the balance or integrity of the nervous system. If the muscle becomes weak when pressed, it's signaling the presence of an imbalance within the body or that its integrity is somehow being compromised.) I found a weak reflex point when I checked Rob's body, but when I held my hand in the "I love you" sign mode, the reflex in his arm instantly became stronger. I didn't realize then the significance of that moment. It would take another three years for all of the pieces of the puzzle to fall into place.

The breakthrough came in the form of an e-mail from a friend containing a picture of one of Dr. Emoto's water crystals—love and gratitude.

Dr. Emoto's water crystal
"Love and gratitude."

When I saw that photograph, it was the first objective representation of what I already knew in my heart to be true—that love and gratitude have the power to heal. That picture became the catalyst for me to link together the experience I had with the "I love you" sign mode and the 12 years of experience I had as a holistic physician trained in chiropractic healing, acupuncture, homeopathy, applied kinesiology (AK), total body modification (TBM), neuro-emotional technique (NET), neuro-linguistic programming (NLP), neuro-modulation technique (NMT), Chinese energetic medicine, natural healing, and aspects of many other forms of energy healing. The result was one unified system that I named "The LifeLine Technique."

Inspired and empowered by Dr. Emoto's work, I've since conducted experiments utilizing a dark-field microscope and live blood-cell analysis to evaluate and document before and after treatments with The LifeLine Technique. These experiments have conclusively demonstrated an instantaneous change in the molecular structure of blood and a dissipation or total elimination of the patient's original symptoms.

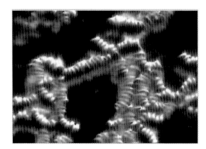

Before: A nine-year-old boy with the symptoms of severe migraine headaches.

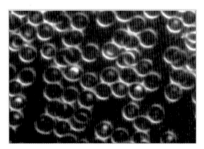

After: Using the power of Infinite Love and Gratitude released his subconscious feelings of anger toward his parents because of their divorce.

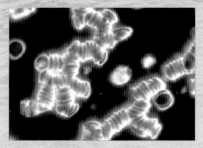

Before: A 32-year-old woman with the symptoms of fibromyalgia.

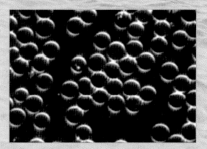

After: Using the power of Infinite Love and Gratitude released the subconscious feelings of grief she had internalized for three years following the death of her mother.

Before: A 40-year-old woman whose attempts to become pregnant had been unsuccessful.

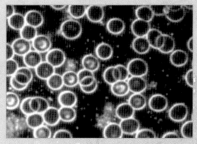

After: Using the power of Infinite Love and Gratitude released the subconscious belief that her age made it impossible for her to get pregnant. She had a baby 11 months later.

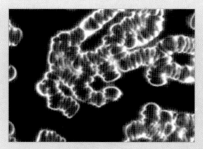

Before: A 42-year-old man with the symptoms of acid reflux.

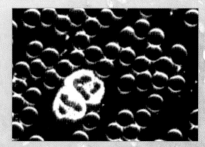

After: Using the power of Infinite Love and Gratitude released subconscious thoughts of shame related to a family situation.

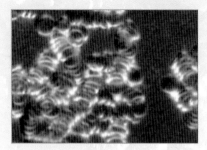

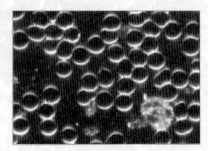

Before: A 53-year-old woman with symptoms of insomnia.

After: Using the power of Infinite Love and Gratitude released subconscious fears about her future provoked by the reorganization of the company where she worked.

THE TRIUNE BRAIN

While the catalyst for my awakening to The LifeLine Technique was Dr. Emoto's water research, its genesis incorporated the work of three other renowned scientists: Dr. Paul MacLean, Dr. Candace Pert, and Dr. Bruce Lipton, whose research further reinforced the hypotheses put forward by Dr. Emoto.

There's a direct link between the brain research of Paul MacLean, M.D., the former director of the National Institute of Mental Health's Laboratory of Brain Evolution and Behavior in Poolesville, Maryland, and Dr. Emoto's water research. The brain is nearly 90 percent water; therefore, its function is directly impacted and influenced by the makeup of that water.

More than 50 years ago, Dr. MacLean, considered to be one of the world's greatest neuroscientists, hypothesized that the skull held not one brain, but three. He referred to this as "the triune brain theory." He noted in his research that the three brains operated like "three interconnected biological computers." He referred to these three brain centers as the neocortex, the limbic system, and the reptilian brain. MacLean believed that each of these was connected by nerves to the other two, but each seemingly operated as its own system with distinct capacities. He considered the harmonious flow of "the triune brain" to be of primary importance for the optimal functioning and health of an individual.

Let me give you a brief description of the function of the triune brain:

- The **neocortex** is the storehouse of higher cognitive functions such as rational thinking and creative expression. This is the part of the brain that separates human beings from other species. It houses our free will, our ability to choose or take action in any given moment.

- The **limbic system** is a storehouse of short-term memory, emotion, attention, instincts, feeding, fighting, fleeing, and sexual behavior. It will trigger a hypnotic state/reptilian response as a means for survival when an overwhelming experience occurs.

- The **reptilian brain**'s purpose is purely survival. It's rigid, obsessive, compulsive, ritualistic, and paranoid. It maintains and regulates all bodily functions ranging from heart rate and respiration to metabolism, immunity, and hormones. There's no conscious choice when a function of the reptilian brain is occurring.

According to the triune brain theory, unification of the three brains enables the electrical frequency of thoughts, feelings, and beliefs to be integrated into behavior. It had previously been assumed that the neocortex, which was believed to be highest level of the brain, dominated the other, lower levels. However, Dr. MacLean's research demonstrated that the limbic system, which *rules emotions,* had the tendency to hijack the higher mental functions whenever necessary for survival, inhibiting emotions from being processed by the neocortex.

In each and every moment, the body receives its instructions for adaptation and regulation from the reptilian brain. These functions are governed via the law of cause and effect. The reptilian brain doesn't have the capacity to learn, only survive. This process is purely mechanistic, and the body isn't able to differentiate between reality and imagination. When a trauma is triggered that's trapped within the limbic brain, a reptilian reaction causes the body to respond as if it were experiencing the situation for the first time. Dr. Emoto's research helps us appreciate how certain emotions can create a physical breakdown in the molecular structure of the water comprising each of the cells within the body. This makes it difficult for the physical life force to flow efficiently.

The body won't break free of reacting in a survival-like fashion until the trauma is processed consciously. From my work with The LifeLine Technique, I've concluded that the limbic system serves as a stopgap, preventing traumatic or shocking experiences from being processed by the neocortex. Instead, the traumatic experience waits to be released, nudging and reminding the body of the unprocessed emotions by "speaking" with symptoms.

Healing and transformation occur when traumatic experiences and emotions are processed to the neocortex, which occurs during sleep, while the eyes are going through rapid eye movement (REM) cycles. This signal of information to the neocortex facilitates a short-term memory to be processed into long-term memory, enabling a person to learn a lesson from a traumatic experience and consequently to live in the present moment.

The LifeLine Technique uses aspects of eye movement desensitization and reprocessing (EMDR) to break limbic-reptilian holding patterns. Using The LifeLine Technique Flow Chart, which has laserlike accuracy, the process is a fast, safe, and non-content way to reconnect to and process emotions. The beauty of the technique is that a person doesn't need to express openly the painful, scary, or challenging emotions; they need only *think* them. When they do, the cells in their body are impacted in the same way that Dr. Emoto's work has demonstrated that water is influenced by its environment.

PROCESSING EMOTIONS ON A MOLECULAR LEVEL

How the body processes emotions has also been studied on a molecular level by Candace Pert, Ph.D. Dr. Pert, a noted researcher and pharmacologist and the author of the books *Molecules of Emotion* and *Everything You Need to Know to Feel Go(o)d,* has proven that neuropeptides—the specific chemicals triggered by emotions—are thoughts converted into matter. *Webster's New World College Dictionary* defines emotions as "complex reactions with *both mental and physical* manifestations" (emphasis mine). Dr. Pert's research discovered that emotions reside in the body and physically interact with cells and tissues. Integrating Dr. Emoto's research with Dr. Pert's discovery of neuropeptides demonstrates the connection between our emotions and our health.

My research has shown me that when emotions are expressed—which is to say that the biochemicals that are the substrate of emotion are flowing freely—all systems are united and made whole. When emotions are repressed, denied, or not allowed to be whatever they may be, our network pathways get blocked, stopping the flow of the vital feel-good, unifying chemicals that run both our biology and behavior.

It's interesting to note that emotions compete for the same receptor sites as heroin. Just as heroin is extremely addictive, so the selectivity of emotional receptors helps us appreciate the addictive quality that dramas have in people's lives. We begin to crave particular emotional experiences as a way of feeding subconscious addictions. So our identity is created by the "network pathways" of emotional addictions.

Just as detoxifying a person from heroin too quickly can be life-threatening, so awakening a person to consciousness without the heightened perception, functional tools, and simple strategies to face the pain, fear, and other challenges of life can inhibit them from being open to change.

Using The LifeLine Technique, we're now able to locate specific neuropeptides blocking the network pathways. By targeting specific traumatic events, limiting beliefs, and symptoms within the subconscious mind and body, we're able to recreate the exact environment of trauma. Once targeted, the intention and frequency of Infinite Love and Gratitude is used while the LifeLine practitioner holds their hand in the sign language mode of "I love you." This process harmonizes and releases the network pathways within the mind and body by affecting the molecular structure of water that makes up each of the cells within the body. Once harmonized and released, the pathways are open, the mind is present, and the body's self-healing capacity takes over.

THE ROLE OF BELIEF

Dr. Bruce Lipton, a cellular biologist and the author of the book *The Biology of Belief,* is the next link in the fusion of science and spirit. His work documents the connection between perception and health. As a result of the research of Drs. Lipton and Emoto, we're now able to recognize and document how the perception of our environment is created by our beliefs. Furthermore, with The LifeLine Technique, we've been able to interpret the exact meaning of symptoms and stress—the language of the subconscious mind— to help us reconnect to what we at one time didn't have the tools or strategies to process. The genetic potential of being able to harmonize limiting beliefs will forever change the way we view genetic processes.

Dr. Lipton set out to discover the brain of a cell. Interestingly, individual cells are like mini-oceans, being composed primarily of water. Dr. Lipton's intention was to find out how perception impacted the function of a cell. He began the process by studying deoxyribonucleic acid, more commonly known as DNA.

DNA was discovered in the early 1950s. This scientific advance was the result of the Nobel Prize–winning work of two scientists, Dr. James Watson and Dr. Francis Crick, based on the initial research done by Dr. Rosalind Franklin. Since that time, scientists have discovered many ways for using the information gleaned from DNA, from genetic fingerprinting to identifying criminals. At the heart of their work has been the belief that DNA is the *brain* of a cell. According to this belief, if people have the genetic makeup for breast cancer, inflammatory bowel disease, or bipolar disorder, they'll eventually develop that disease. As a consequence, some women are having complete bilateral, radical mastectomies without any physical sign of cancer due to a genetic evaluation of their DNA.

The tragedy, as Dr. Lipton's research has documented, is that DNA is *not* the brain of the cell. Dr. Lipton conducted tests in which he removed the nucleus of a cell containing the DNA. He hypothesized that if DNA were the brain of a cell, something very predictable would happen when it was removed—the cell would die instantly, just as a person would die if their brain were removed. Just the opposite occurred: The cell lived. Dr. Lipton then began to remove the individual components of a cell one at a time until he found the specific anatomical part that resulted in instantaneous death. He discovered that the brain of a cell was its protein receptors.

Protein receptors are very thin membranes that function like a cell-phone antenna, sending messages directly to the nucleus. They're not only on the outside of a cell and the nucleus, but also in our senses—that is, the rods and cones in our eyes and the cilia (hairs) in our nose and ears. All of our sensory receptors are made of protein. And in an antenna-type fashion, protein picks up the vibratory frequencies of sound and light and sends the signals to our brain. Depending upon the message, the brain then sends a signal down the spinal cord to specific areas of the body.

When the protein receptors on the outsides of individual cells receive the information via *neuropeptides,* they send a signal to the nucleus, where the messages are encoded. From that encoding, the protein *creates* the DNA for a specific cell so that it will adapt to its environment. The nucleus, according to Dr. Lipton's research, is in fact the reproductive system of a cell—it is the center of a cell's ability to regenerate.

Dr. Lipton's exhaustive studies also sought to find out how a cell responds to stimuli, in a similar fashion to the way the brain reacts to the senses. He wanted to know how the liver, lungs, or intestines react to what's going on in the external environment.

What he discovered, as explained in his book, was the link between beliefs and the state of health: "Cellular biologists now recognize that the environment (external universe and internal physiology), and more importantly our perception of the environment, directly controls the activity of our genes."

When it comes down to it, we'll only perceive what we believe, and our beliefs have a direct impact on the molecular structure of the water that makes up every cell, organ, and system of our body. Dr. Emoto's water-crystal research mirrors how the perception of the "external universe" directly impacts the molecular structure of water, the same water that makes up the "internal physiology" of the body.

The LifeLine Technique creates a conscious awareness of both the "external environment" and the "internal physiology" by harmonizing and releasing limiting beliefs trapped within the subconscious mind. Water's molecular structure is enhanced as our consciousness begins to expand. Not until the subconscious is made conscious are we able to choose or take action based on what we're truly experiencing in any given moment. The ramifications are infinite. Creating inner peace makes it possible to create world peace.

INFINITE LOVE AND GRATITUDE

Using a symptom as the portal, the LifeLine practitioner is able to use the LifeLine Flow Chart to discover the specific subconscious emotional patterns of disconnection and instantly harmonize these imbalances with the frequency of Infinite Love and Gratitude. As with Dr. Emoto's water-crystal research, these profound words have a direct influence on the molecular structure of the body. Defining "Infinite Love and Gratitude" helps us appreciate why.

From time and the cosmos to the cycle of the seasons and life itself, the universe is infinite. It's forever expanding and undefined. Therefore, as a being of the universe, your mind possesses the nature and potential of the infinite. The infinite universe and mind are the great frontier, the endless entity of boundless mystery.

Acknowledging your connection to the infinite universe and the infinite mind is fundamental to understanding the unlimited potential that you possess. This view is magnified to infinity by the core truth that you're a spiritual being having a human-being experience. By "be-ing," you experience the infinite essence and wonder of life.

It has been said that there are only two true emotions, love and fear. All other feelings are an extension of these two. However, love takes precedence, for it's only when love is absent that fear is present.

The experience of fear is a gift. True fear happens in a moment of danger and then is immediately released. It's a survival mechanism that's governed by the reptilian brain. The end result of living a life in a constant state of fear is victimization and suffering. Louise L. Hay, the author of many best-selling books, including *You Can Heal Your Life*, is the matriarch of teaching people to love themselves. She has helped millions around the world with this simple yet profound concept. She so eloquently states, "If you change your thoughts, you change your reality." As Dr. Emoto has demonstrated, choosing to love, accept, and forgive unconditionally is universally the most powerful healing energy.

We give thanks to individuals or experiences that we value. However, what about the painful, scary, and challenging people and experiences in our lives? By embracing them with the "attitude of gratitude," we're acknowledging them as having worth. Value gives life meaning, and with meaning we're able to transcend victimization and suffering. The most powerful people throughout all of history have endured the most difficult situations. A belief structure that every challenge is an opportunity for growth or a vehicle for spiritual awakening empowers a person to move through life in a heroic fashion. We all have the capacity to be heroes—to move through the painful and scary experiences of life with faith, courage, and determination—and to trust that everything happens for a reason, even if we don't understand the meaning in the moment. It all begins with the power of Infinite Love and Gratitude.

For the past five years, I've been teaching seminars internationally to both laypersons and healing-arts professionals. The philosophy of The LifeLine Technique is simple to understand. It combines the best of natural-healing modalities into a unified system that transforms the core emotions trapped within the subconscious mind. Just like the transformation of distilled water into various crystals, the change occurs instantaneously within the mind and body. We continue to document The LifeLine Technique and the power of Infinite Love and Gratitude with live blood-cell analysis and have repeatedly found that both a person's perception of their environment and the function of their internal physiology are transformed.

Let me share an example in which the documentation was provided by the patient's medical doctor, with before and after reports. In the summer and early fall of 2003, a patient I'll refer to as "Alice" began experiencing uterine bleeding and abdominal pains. The lower area of her stomach was also protruding. At first Alice, who was 51 at the time, thought she might be pregnant. Instead, a gynecological exam and subsequent biopsies revealed three ovarian cysts and a fibroid tumor the size of a grapefruit. The masses were all found to be benign.

Alice came to see me shortly after the diagnosis. I knew that with The LifeLine Technique we would be able to determine the *root* cause of why her subconscious mind was using the *symptoms* of a fibroid tumor and ovarian cysts to communicate. But to help facilitate the healing process, Alice had to take responsibility. I discussed with her the importance of following the Five Basics of Optimal Health—the proper quantity, quality, and frequency of water, food, rest, and exercise and owning her power.

As we continued to work together, the abdominal bleeding and pain ceased, and ultrasound and sonogram tests showed that the masses were shrinking. Despite that, Alice's gynecologist believed that they should be surgically removed.

On the day that Alice was scheduled to have the cysts removed, the operating room was overbooked. After waiting eight-and-a-half hours for the surgical appointment, she chose to leave the hospital. She later told me that she accepted the opinion of her doctor;

however, she'd been to a LifeLine seminar and knew in her heart that her body had the power to heal itself.

During a subsequent treatment using The LifeLine Technique, Alice's subconscious mind revealed a limiting belief being held in her root chakra dating back to the age of 12 and associated with the emotions of regret, guilt, and fear. I asked her to pay attention to what *immediately* came to mind when I said those words aloud. This is what she told me:

> Immediately, my thoughts went back to the time I was awakened by an argument between my parents. It was the first time I'd ever heard them raise their voices to each other. The next thing I knew, my father was standing above me with a knife raised over my head. But when he looked me in the eye, he stopped. He attacked my sister instead, stabbing her to death in front of me. . . .
>
> I thought my father hadn't hurt me because I'd looked him in the eye; and I believe that if I'd awakened my sister, she, too, might still be alive. I always felt guilty that I survived and my sister didn't. Subconsciously, I felt remorse, guilt, regret, and fear for not having the courage and presence of mind to wake her up.
>
> Reflecting on my experience of the treatment with The LifeLine Technique, I came to accept and appreciate the strength and purpose of lives such as my sister's that were so unfairly and suddenly cut short. As a result of the treatment, I've experienced an inner sense of peace and confidence and now resolve to forgive myself, and commit on a much deeper level to my well-being in all areas of my life and relationships.

Over the next nine months, Alice made conscientious efforts to follow the Five Basics of Optimal Health and continued weekly treatments. In August 2005, tests indicated that her uterus had returned to normal size and that all of the masses were gone.

RECONNECTING TO OUR POWER

The LifeLine Technique consciously reconnects us to the power of our thoughts, feelings, and choices. If you have the belief that everything is an opportunity, no matter how challenging or difficult, your mind will send that positive charge to the water that makes up the molecular structure of the cells in your body.

It's common to think, *If I can just find the right person/job/other external solution, then everything will be just fine.* However, if we don't change ourselves, we'll continue to repeat the same relationships, financial challenges, and health issues over and over again. Not until we become conscious of the limiting beliefs and the emotions that are trapped within the survival aspects of our subconscious mind will we begin to recognize that other choices exist. These patterns are the language of the subconscious mind that can now be easily understood and transformed with The LifeLine Technique and the power of Infinite Love and Gratitude. The LifeLine Technique demonstrates the healing power of water and quantifies the limitless potential all people possess to heal, find inner peace, and create harmony in their environments.

The LifeLine Law of Transformation and Creation states: Emotions transform energy; energy creates movement; movement is change; and change is the essence of life. It's the *fear* of change that keeps people stuck in patterns of victimization and suffering. The process of healing is a spiritual path, the evolutionary journey to awakening your spirit. Dr. Emoto's research has courageously paved the way for the fusion of science and spirit.

○ ○ ○

FURTHER INFORMATION

For further information on The LifeLine Technique, see: **www.infiniteloveandgratitude.com**.

○ ○ ○   ○ ○ ○

CHAPTER 8

DOWSING FOR WATER

by Sig Lonegren

Today, dowsing is used for many different purposes—health, earth energies, oil, archaeology, and many more. However, by far the most important target for diviners is water. Until recently in Britain, a liter of water cost more than the same amount of gas in the U.S.! Many feel that the major battles of the 21st century won't be over oil, but over an even more basic commodity: water.

Hydrologists explain that all water comes from the sky as rain and then goes through the well-known cycle of falling on the land, going into rivers and flowing into lakes and oceans, where it evaporates up to the skies, only to fall again as rain. This is called "secondary water," because it's used over and over again. Dowsers find that in addition to this source, there's another one. It's "primary water" that comes from deep in the earth and is the result of the chemical processes going on down there. For example, when you mix an acid and a base (especially under heat and pressure), you get a salt plus water. And where does this primary or "juvenile" water go when under heat and pressure? It moves away, toward the surface, through any crack it can find. It gathers to form enormous underground rivers deep in the bowels of the earth; and when it finds a crack in the ceiling, it goes upward again in what American dowsers call a "dome" and British dowsers call a "blind spring." When it very occasionally reaches the surface, it's called a "geyser." But in most cases, its upward journey is halted upon reaching an impermeable layer (such as clay), and so it spreads out laterally as veins. From above, this looks like a spider with an odd number of legs.

Most holy wells come from this primary water. In addition to H_2O, many of them have other elements mixed in as well. At the Chalice Well in Glastonbury, England, for example, the water is called "chalybeate." While it runs clear, it's full of iron. Across the road, the White Spring is full of calcium [see Chapter 17].

Well above the timberline and only a short distance from the top of Mount Katahdin in Maine, where the sun first hits the United States each morning, is a spring of water. Above it is only hard rock. So where does that water come from? It can't be rainwater percolating down from above. It's primary water, and it comes from way below the base of that impressive mountain. The message here is that while we're facing a critical shortage of secondary water around our planet, there are ample supplies of primary or juvenile water that dowsers can find for us.

No dowser hits water 100 percent of the time, but there are water-well dowsers in California who consistently have success year after year between 85 and 95 percent of the time. Not only can they tell their clients exactly where to put the drill bit in, but how deep they'll have to go and how many gallons a minute they'll get!

Dowsing is a practice that enhances our intuition and can connect us to sources of information that can't be found through rational methods. Until relatively recently in our history, diviners were burned at the stake. But one form of divination was judged too important to include in this witch hunt, and that was water dowsing. Despite sometimes being referred to as "water witching," it was just too valuable a skill to wipe off the face of Europe, as happened with so many other uses of this ancient art.

It's only within the past half-century that these other applications have been rediscovered. And it's amazing how many of them are also directly connected to veins and domes of primary water. For example, domes of primary water are found underneath all ancient sacred sites. This was first noted by Reginald Allendar Smith, who worked for the British Museum and in 1925 became the Trustee Representative on the Ancient Monuments Board for England. After he retired in the 1930s, he was one of the first to publish articles in the *British Society of Dowsers Journal* stating that he had dowsed water under all of the ancient sacred sites that were also attracting the attention of ley hunters. (One can commit any heresy after retiring!) According to the theory of ley lines, the water is yin, and the energy leys—six- to eight-foot wide straight beams of energy that cross at power centers directly over the yin veins or domes of water—are yang.

Likewise, information about many archaeological sites can be enhanced by seeing their relationship—or lack thereof—to water. For example, most Bronze Age hut circles in Britain weren't built over primary water.

In terms of health, German dowsers found in the 1920s that certain houses had a high incidence of cancer—*Krebs Häuser* (cancer houses). And under these houses, but not their neighbors', they found crossings of underground veins of water.

It seems that it is the *flow* rather than the water itself that's associated with many forms of degenerative disease. Drinking-water dowsers, who open themselves up to these energies, can frequently be seen wearing copper bracelets to help ease the pain of arthritis. Many alternative-health practitioners find that all their work can be undone if their patient goes home after a treatment and sleeps over underground water crossings. Again, it's the flow that seems to cause the problems. (Primary water, once it reaches the surface of the earth, is usually perfectly fine to drink.)

So underground water plays an important part in many areas of dowsing. It can contribute to contracting disease, and it can enhance the possibility of connection with the numinous at sacred spaces; but it's the ability to find good sources of primary water that will be dowsers' major contribution to the 21st century.

◇ ◇ ◇

RESOURCE RECOMMENDATIONS

Sig Lonegren, *Spiritual Dowsing,* Bloomington, Indiana: authorHouse, 1986, reprinted 2004. History of earth energies, healing and other uses of dowsing today. A book for the spiritual pilgrim.

Sig Lonegren's Website (lots of information about water and dowsing): **www.geomancy.org**

If you want to learn how to dowse, check out:

- The American Society of Dowsers, **www.dowsers.org**
- The British Society of Dowsers: **www.britishdowsers. org**
- Dowsing organizations around the world: **www. britishdowsers.org/groups_2a.html**

◊◊◊ ◊◊◊

CHAPTER 9

LISTENING TO WATER

by Miranda Alcott

S haring water with the firefighters, EMTs, police officers, and chaplains at what was left of the World Trade Center after September 11 created some of the most sacred moments of my life.

What brought us all together was a few simple bottles of water available at designated spots on the site. I wondered if anyone standing around the flats of bottled water in exhausted silence was aware of the healing properties of the liquid they were holding. They were replenishing what had been lost due to extreme stress in their already fatigued bodies. They took giant trusting gulps as we stood amid the rubble and body parts. Were they drinking to quench their thirst . . . or to put out their emotional flames?

I'm a crisis responder, intuitive healer, and counselor with a master's degree in spiritual psychology. But most important, I'm a listener. Together with my service hearing/crisis intervention canine, Whisper, in my daily practice I work with people who are confronting some form of crisis in their lives. They may have deep issues—recent or sudden deaths in their families, exposure to mass critical incidents, diagnoses of terminal illness, and life-direction decisions—or the simple yet overwhelming physical toll of everyday stress.

My work allows me to experience many different energetics in places and with those I go to help. Many of the things I observe aren't visible to most people. I'm able to experience, listen, and see energetic fields, colors, frequencies, and vibrations that most others aren't aware of.

I do this by using what's currently referred to as a *holographic paradigm,* which includes *quanta,* or small groupings of energy. These groupings in turn make up atoms that resonate at individual frequencies. At an infinitesimal level of existence, energetically, we're all a part of the whole; but each atom's frequencies are so unique that every one of us carries a very individual energetic "snowflake." What I experience are the different "signatures" that constitute the fields that permeate and surround each of us and, in fact, all living organisms.

Some of these energetic "nets" of wavelike structures appear as diaphanous forms that make themselves visible to me in a floating manner. They can be created by many events—violent crime, a natural disaster, or simply by the laughter of children. Some result from simple tones of music, which put on a light show the likes of which can only be rivaled by the aurora borealis. (There are more complete examples in my soon-to-be-published book, *An Extraordinary Journey Through an Ordinary World.*) Other energies I see are those that are working 24/7 to keep our bodies running at top efficiency. "Looking" at these energetic forms and fields, in combination with the energetic directives I receive, allows me to access the information from which I work.

My conscious association with water has been going on for quite some time. At two and a half years old, I watched one morning as a pool of water reached up to help a bird rinse its feathers. And early in my life I noticed that although most animals drank lots of water, there were some people who didn't drink much, if any. I didn't understand this, and for a very long time couldn't imagine refueling my body without water's presence. I watched water around these individuals, but didn't see any answers until years later in my private practice, when I noticed that the people who spoke of the mental, physical, emotional, or spiritual abuses in their lives were the same ones who usually wouldn't open the bottle of water I offer at the beginning of each session.

In observing my clients' interactions with the water offered, I saw that there were some who accepted it as a social gesture, some who fondled it in contemplative moments, and some who drank the entire bottle as soon as they could get the top off. When I would ask how they felt about interacting with the water, each of them seemed to hold the belief that drinking, ingesting, or holding it would, at that moment, somehow intensify their own issues. I also noticed that some would began their de-stressing processes almost as soon as they were offered the water. From then on, I used water as an active participant when called out into the field for my crisis-response work.

One of my earliest experiences with water out in the field was during an emergency response at our local airport. I saw a woman in physical distress who had fields of faintly colored energy surrounding her body. These colors were rapidly fading in and out. The closer I got to her, the more I felt my blood sugar lower. She was holding a foam cup filled with what I assumed was juice, as the energies rolling off the surface of the cup were of a pale organic orange. As I got closer to her, I noticed that the cup was filled with water. How could water, which normally emits many colors, be emitting only one color? The woman's energetic field was so faint and mottled that I quickly called a nurse over.

Later that afternoon the nurse sought me out to tell me that the woman was a diabetic and had been experiencing a diabetic collapse. The water had been reflecting what she'd needed earlier: orange juice.

WATER AS HEALER

The effects of water's presence in our lives are so obvious that many of us take them for granted, yet we've all noticed how excited children become when they interact with this substance. It also has its own character. Have you ever noticed, when entering an empty room, that if there's a pitcher of water in it, you don't feel alone?

We take water with us everywhere these days. When we're hiking or exercising, we carry bottles of it for regeneration and rejuvenation. We're created in water, bathe in it, cleanse wounds with it, and can die when we don't have enough of it. With roughly two-thirds of our planet covered by water and our bodies containing similar proportions of it, is it any wonder that it's such an amazing conduit for our thoughts, energies, and healing?

Nature provides so many ways for us to live more easily if we can only be more sensitive to what surrounds us, and animals can be such great teachers for us all. Recently, I stood in the high mountains of New Mexico while the lightning-filled charcoal clouds announced a coming storm. As the ions increased, I watched a beautiful coal-black stallion prancing to discharge the intensity of the electromagnetic energy. He did this by tossing his head, arching his tail, and bucking himself off the ground, breaking the build-up of static electricity. He instinctively knew what he needed to do in order to release the accumulation of the converging energies. When the rain clouds broke, he calmed, and water soothed his body.

I believe that we have a primordial relationship with water as our earliest parent—one of the life forces from which we sprang. It can be so comforting, while also having an uncanny ability to reflect emotions. The reason for this, as I understand it, is that thoughts are energy, which creates vibrations. These can have color and distinct forms, all of which I see. There are also more hues than we perceive with our eyes, including what I call "colorless colors." When water's healthy, I experience it as a glowing liquid light that hums. Vibrations give me information, and once I have that, I wait for an energy flow, or "energetic directive," to see how I'm supposed to help.

As a listener, I naturally pay attention to most beings. In April 2003, my service dog, Whisper, reacted very strongly to the photographs of water crystals that Dr. Emoto was displaying during one of his presentations in Los Angeles. She reacted to both his crystal images and to the vibrations of his tuning fork. Whisper is a healer in her own right, and she was deeply affected by the communication that she saw in Dr. Emoto's pictures. Her reaction was one of surprise, as she looked at the huge images displayed on the screen. I watched her as she stared at each slide, appearing to communicate with some of the images. At one in particular, she sat upright and was visibly moved. I was deeply touched by the photographs; and it occurred to me then, after so many years of working with water, how patient it is with us all.

Dr. Emoto gave me his card, and when Whisper and I saw him speak once again in Santa Fe several months later, he asked us to participate in his next book. We were thrilled!

The following December, Dr. Emoto came to one of my evening intuitive presentations. I asked anyone wishing to work with me to choose one of the bowls of water located in the back of the room. They were instructed to place their most pressing issue or question, in thought form, into the kindness of the water.

A red-haired woman of about 35 gave me her first name, handed me her bowl of water and stood off to my side, motionless. After a few moments, the vibrational patterns and colors in the water became apparent to me. I watched as its energetic field made clear what she needed to know. The surface of the liquid was acting like a screen, reflecting her inner confusion, deep fear, and physical illness. I could see by looking at the energies surrounding her body that this physical illness was manifesting itself as tension in her musculoskeletal system: bones, muscles, and joints.

As I worked with her nonverbally, I could see that the energy, colors, and vibrations emanating from her body were becoming more vibrant. I then verbally relayed to her what was taking place currently in her life. As I spoke to her about how she could dispel

Above: Miranda with her dog, Whisper.

her physical issues, she and the water began to take on more of each other's properties, appearing more and more similar. A woman and a bowl of water, which had started as two distinctive elements, were now experiencing an energetic exchange.

Being hearing impaired, I use a sign language interpreter. With the lights in my eyes I couldn't see the woman's face, so I looked at my interpreter to see if she had any questions or needed to say anything. My interpreter had no signs for me, so I continued.

I saw that the woman's body was wrapped in fields of fearful emotional energies. They were encasing her chest area and causing some restrictive breathing patterns. In checking for any kind of genetic illness, I saw that the tightness in her chest came from a current emotional situation, which was the cause of her fear.

Happily, she remained receptive for the entire time I worked with her, and I could see the colors and energies surrounding her body shifting. Simultaneously, so were the energies and colors of the bowl of water. Her innate self-altering processes were affecting the water inside her body, which in turn was resonating with the water in the bowl. Even though she was no longer physically holding the bowl, they were inextricably connected. The water revealed that her life would be taking a new direction and that her deep fear of this change was contributing to her physical illness. I let her know that it was imperative that she understand that her illness was very possibly of her own creation. She thanked me and wept as she returned to her seat.

Several weeks later I crossed paths with the woman again. She told me that she'd always been unable to deal with stress and had recently been hired for a new job and was feeling very uncertain if it would end up taking over her life. She said that after I worked with her, the pain in her joints had stopped and the tension in the rest of her body had been released. She told me that ever since that night, she has never looked at water in the same way.

At another one of my evening presentations, a man in his late 40s came and stood next to me in silence and handed me his bowl of water. What I saw in it was that he wanted to know what was wrong with his health. I could see that he was incredibly tense, with ruddy fields of opaque energy, which pointed to his health condition possibly being chronic. When I suggested that spending time floating in water might help him, the look on his face was one of disdain as he returned to his seat.

Several months later, in a local market, his wife introduced herself and told me how grateful she was that they'd come that evening. She said her husband had been going to doctors who'd prescribed several medications and told him that unless he took them, he'd become very sick. The man hadn't listened to them and hadn't taken the drugs. Although he was fairly certain that water couldn't help him in any way, either, his wife told me that after my presentation, he'd gone home and spent considerably more time floating in their pool. A few months later when he went for his next medical appointment, the doctor was pleased to see that his blood pressure had dropped significantly and commended him on finally taking the prescribed medication. As his wife tells it, her husband just laughed and said, "Actually, all I did was float in water."

The "floating man" and the union between the red-haired woman and the small bowl of water reminded me of the small bottles of water in the large hands of those men at Ground Zero. But what was the water actually doing for the people at Ground Zero? Watching as they used it to rinse the dust from their masks and the grime from their eyes and tilted their heads back to take a drink, I saw that each of them went into a place that was soothing for them. Whether that was a precious memory of their family, a special vacation, or their kids' faces, water had become a portal to a rare moment of reprieve from their horrific surroundings. Taking a simple drink had created a sacred moment with a great healer.

EXERCISE TO FACILITATE LISTENING TO WATER

If you'd like to connect with the healing power of water, just sit quietly for a moment and "hear" its sound. In your mind's eye, see a form of water that you enjoy experiencing: a breezy mountain lake, a reflection of fall leaves in a puddle, a large rushing river, a beautiful city fountain, a salty ocean, a desert monsoon sky, or a high-mountain snow pool. Watch these images in your head. Can you feel the changes inside you as the water in your body "recognizes" the vision of the water that you're seeing? What are you physically experiencing as these elements resonate with each other? Is the rhythm of your body altering slightly?

In your stillness, what can you hear water telling you? Become quiet and still and allow your entire body to "listen" to its whispers. Whatever it has told you is very powerful guidance. What you do with this wisdom depends on what your commitment to your life is.

Once you've received your gift, you'll continue to hear the flow of water as it gently takes a place in your heart. Don't be surprised if your dreams also bring you healing messages from water.

○○○ ○○○

CHAPTER 10

THE WATERS OF LIFE

by Carrie Jost

Water is a mystery—a mystery we can feel when we yearn to be by the sea, a river, or a lake when the weather is hot. Its presence balances the heat and reminds us that all life began in water. It speaks to our bodies. Within those bodies are the counterparts of the waters of Earth: the oceans of salty water that bathe every cell; the rivers and streams, which direct the three major fluids to the parts of the body that need them; the lakes and pools of the organs, which hold the reservoirs and inform the senses. Just like Earth, we, too, are 75 percent water.

Water is feminine. It curves and moves in spirals, vortexes, and figure eights. It's also in a state of constant motion. If it becomes still, it stagnates and attracts the energy of decay and disease. The water within our bodies is also in constant motion, moving in the same ways as that of the Earth. Water is both life giving and life sustaining.

Water is able to grow and expand. It's also able to dissolve and expel solid particles. It's important that it has the ability to cleanse and purify itself. A lively mountain stream can expel the dissolved particles from a rotting sheep within 150 yards.

ENERGY IN MOTION

We begin our lives in a sac of water, a warm ocean that's constantly rocking the new life within it. The fetus is at one with this sea, nurtured and supported through the waters of the mother's womb. This is the baby's first experience of receiving information, which is transmitted via the surrounding waters and the fluids along the umbilical cord. It's apparent to me from my healing work with clients that the mother's feelings are also transmitted through this medium. Trauma and shock will unsettle the fetus, while love, acceptance, and other positive feelings will nurture it.

Over the years, it has become clear that water is affected by the subtlest of vibrations, including emotional states. Blessed water is at the heart of many spiritual traditions and is known to have healing properties. Now we have the findings from Emoto's work to show us visually the direct effect that emotions have on water—they change its structure. Positive thoughts and feelings create the most beautiful of frozen pictures, while negative ones result in distortion and discoloration. This is water receiving and transmitting information at an emotional level.

Emotion, or "e-motion," can be seen as energy in motion. Water in the body—whether it's the great ocean that bathes every cell; the rivers of blood, lymph, and cerebrospinal fluid; the little streams of the capillaries and minor nerves; or the great lakes of the stomach and the pools of the eyes—can stop functioning optimally if there isn't enough of it or if it becomes too still. [See Chapter 6.] When our emotions are unacknowledged or

unexpressed, they, too, can become stuck and suppressed in a part of the body. [See Chapter 7.] They may consolidate into thoughts or belief systems, which then become patterns of thinking and behaving. From my experience, this is likely to occur in the fluids of the body and may result in disease, chronic conditions, and illness. We know from the work begun by Louise L. Hay that many biochemical problems and disease states have an emotional aspect that has often gone unrecognized.

DEHYDRATION

What happens when we become dehydrated? Dr. Fereydoon Batmanghelidj says that in his experience, "It is chronic water shortage in the body that causes most diseases of the human body." When we lack water, we lose our vital connection with this life-giving substance, and the result is stress in our physical systems. All the fluids of the body become affected, the information transmission is scrambled, and we no longer work efficiently on all levels. Without sufficient water, we're not allowing the fluid intelligence of life to nurture and sustain us.

For example, when we're learning new things, the brain uses up a lot of water by connecting to what it already knows, adding the fresh information, and attempting to make conscious what may at first be beneath consciousness. Drinking extra water helps hugely in the learning process. This has been tried in schools and other learning environments with great success.

The nervous system, including the brain, operates in the cerebrospinal fluid. If this part of the body is lacking in water, then the brain and nervous system go into a stressed state. Anxiety, panic, tension, difficulty with learning, and even clumsiness can result. Ironically, the stress itself can cause further dehydration, as the nervous system needs more water to cope with any new situation.

We can apply our understanding of water in a metaphorical way to the fluids of the body. We can easily check if a person is dehydrated by using kinesiological muscle testing. This can tell us the location of the problem, how it's affecting the system, and the trigger that set it off in the first place. Old traumas, shock, ongoing emotional states, and other difficulties may all trigger imbalances.

A young woman came to see me because she was suffering from anxiety, panic attacks, and asthmatic breathing. I found that she wasn't dehydrated overall. She knew the value of drinking six or seven glasses of water a day. She knew not to count tea, coffee, and fruit juice as water, since the body treats them as food. Nevertheless, we found that her nervous system was dehydrated. For some reason, her body wasn't absorbing water in this area. Using kinesiology, I tracked the source of the problem and we found that the trigger was a trauma in her family some years before. She remembered that her asthma had started then (this condition can be one of the signs of dehydration in the body).

A potent approach to healing is to witness the trigger, accept it, and then find the appropriate energy technique to restore balance, health, and vitality. Here, we used energy techniques to restore the young woman's nervous system to a state of full hydration. She didn't even need to drink any more water than before. After the treatment, her anxiety and panic decreased and her wheeziness disappeared. She was able to move forward in her life, leaving the trauma behind her.

THE WATER ELEMENT

When water spirals, it's making the movement of creation. All growth takes place in a spiral. Watch a fern unfurl, a bean grow out of the ground, or the petals of a rose unfold, and you'll see this spiraling motion in operation.

The DNA in the center of each of our cells is a spiral—a double helix that carries our inheritance. Ancestral influences are passed on through it and also through the water element, according to ancient Chinese tradition. The emerging science of epigenetics is now showing us that we not only inherit physical traits (such as size, eye color, and tendencies toward particular diseases), but also emotional states. These are often held in the water element and in particular in the kidney meridian, one of the paths of energy that run through the body.

A young man came to see me wanting to be more confident and to take the next step on his path in life. He found it hard to think positively about himself and felt held back by his anxiety about change. We discovered that his DNA and kidney meridian were low in energy. (Kidney energy problems often manifest as anxiety or fear.) Muscle testing showed that he'd inherited an emotional pattern from his father, and that it reached back in his ancestry for 16 generations. The pattern was one of anxiety and fear about change and moving on in life—exactly what he was experiencing. He also recognized this in his father. An additional pattern from his mother, who'd been anxious about giving birth to her son, was also affecting his kidney energy.

By working with the energy of the kidney meridian, we were able to restore balance to the DNA and the water element, and then hydration became optimal in every system in the young man's body. Now free of the pattern of fear and anxiety, he found a spiritual teacher, made changes in his way of life, and began to feel good about himself.

The water element in many ancient traditions is the one that relates to nourishing and nurturing. In the Native American tradition, Father Sun brings his love and passion to Mother Earth, who receives this; and together they give birth to their daughter

Water, a Goddess and the Spirit of the plants, who brings life and beauty to the earth. It seems that we in the West have forgotten the ancient stories and the beauty of honoring the balance of nature that we can still see in other cultures.

The first acupuncture point on the kidney meridian on the bottom of the feet is called "Bubbling Spring." It's a major point for energy input. When we walk, this part of the foot acts as a pump and encourages the waters of the body to move. It's natural for them to circulate and, as already mentioned, if they become too still, they turn stagnant. To encourage movement, we can walk, run, or do whatever activity we enjoy. Figure eights will spiral the body's waters into motion and energize them. So by circling the body, we can enhance our flexibility and the flow of our waters. Belly dancers know this!

A woman who was having eye problems, with fuzzy sight and a slight gritty feeling in her eyes, came to a seminar I gave about kinesiological ways of working with water. I see the eyes as two of the lakes in the body. For a lake to stay healthy, it needs a throughput of water. So we muscle checked and found that figure eights would be a helpful remedy for this woman. She rolled her eyes in a sideways "eight" movement, and then went on to move both her eyes and her neck in this way for a short time. Afterward, her sight became clear, her eyes looked brighter, and the gritty feeling disappeared.

THE MEMORY OF WATER

"I know it in my waters" is an old saying. It may be accurate, when we consider that water has a memory. It recalls what it's like to be healthy and strives for this state of perfection in its motion. It also remembers subtle energies that have passed through it.

The memory is actually a vibration. This can be very powerful—when information in the form of a vibration is introduced into the body, it can bring about healing to the entire system. Homeopathy works in this way, using the power of water to absorb and retain information that has been shaken into it. Flower essences, pioneered by Dr. Edward Bach, work in a similar manner, using the vibration of flowers in water to trigger self-healing. [See Chapter 20.]

The waters in the body are always ready to receive information from the environment. We continually receive and give out information through our sensory organs and also through our chakra system (the word *chakra* from the Sanskrit for *wheel*). These wheels of energy are vortexes, which are linked to the nervous and hormonal systems. They act as gateways from the subtle realms to the physical and from the body to the environment. In this way, we're connected to all life.

The common factor here seems to be water. As we bring information into our bodies, our fluids pick up the data and send them to the relevant part of the system. Messages will also be sent out to the world around us. This will give us a particular kind of reception from the people we're with. Within the body, a similar system is in operation. Here, our waters are affected by the signals we give ourselves. Messages of love, appreciation, or kindness will affect us in a positive way, while negative feedback will eventually cause problems with our well-being.

Over the years of working in the field of natural therapies, I've become more and more aware of the importance of water. It's an obvious factor in creating and maintaining health and well-being. Increasing research, including that outlined above, has pointed out that the way we treat water, in the world and within our bodies, is significant both for our own health and that of the planet.

We're all looking for vitality, happiness, and good health; and we have an ally: water. Once we acknowledge this and recognize its nurturing and healing powers, we can begin to feel it working for and with us. Water ties us all to each other and to every other life form on Earth. We could begin by feeling connected to each part of ourselves.

WATER TIPS

- Drink six to ten glasses a day—more if you're learning, and more if you're stressed.

- If drinking a minimum of six glasses a day, take some salt to balance the water.

- Start the day with one or two glasses of water to flush the system and bring new life to your day.

- Drink deeply to energize and feed the water element in your body.

- Sip slowly to detox and cleanse.

- Hold the water in your mouth for a few seconds to encourage absorption.

- Dechlorinate tap water by letting it stand in a jug—the chlorine will evaporate.

- Energize water by stirring it, blessing it, or using a water-energizing device.

- Move your internal water pump: Run, walk, move your ankles, and do any other foot or leg movement that you enjoy.

- Get a foot massage.

- Circle the body—move in figure eights with your eyes, head, hips, and shoulders.

- Heal scars by moving your hand in a figure eight over them.

- Talk kindly to yourself (and your inner waters) with appreciation, respect, and acceptance.

- Speak to others in the same way.

◌ ◌ ◌

FURTHER READING

Olof Alexandersson, *Living Water,* Gateway Books, 1997.

Fereydoon Batmanghelidj, *Your Body's Many Cries for Water,* Global Health Solutions, 1997.

Callum Coats, *Living Energies,* Gateway Books, 1998.

Candace B. Pert, Ph.D., *Molecules of Emotion,* Scribner, 1999.

Michel Schiff, *The Memory of Water,* Thorsons, 1994.

Peter van Oosterum, *Tears: A Key to a Remedy,* Ashgrove Press, 1997.

FURTHER INFORMATION

See: **www.creativekinesiology.org**

◌ ◌ ◌   ◌ ◌ ◌

PART III

Spiritual and Mythological Perspectives

INTRODUCTION

W ater has been revered over thousands of years for its powerful spiritual qualities. In the following chapters, we'll see how this respect is a common theme in many of the world's religions, and how water is used both for sacramental purposes and in stories for teaching the faith.

Animism is the oldest spiritual path, dating back to the earliest times, and José Luis Stevens's paper gives a glimpse into an era when the spirits of local rivers, lakes, and seas were universally revered. Their help and guidance were essential to early humans' very survival in a dangerous world.

Starhawk continues in a similar vein, with her deep understanding of paganism and its rituals.

Other authors explore how water is central in many major religious traditions, including Hinduism, Christianity, and Judaism. All have the common theme of the powerful cleansing and purifying properties that water possesses and its centrality in the processes of redemption and forgiveness, as well as initiation into faith.

The spirit of place, especially important for understanding spirituality and water, is also a concept that several of these papers have in common. In many cultures, ancient and modern, the powers of water are believed to be especially strong in certain locations—such as the sacred river Ganges in India, one drop of which is said to cleanse the soul of all karma. In the same vein, Doreen Virtue describes the goddesses and presiding female saints of Lourdes and other holy places, Richard Beaumont writes about the Roman spa of Bath in England, and William Bloom explores the Chalice Well of Glastonbury.

Maril Crabtree's essay ends this section (and the book) practically and inspiringly, with a range of ideas and rituals for readers to try themselves, from simply drinking a glass of water or taking a shower with awareness and appreciation, to techniques for healing illness.

What's most astonishing about this collection of essays is the remarkable unity that so many diverse traditions display in their perception of water over countless ages. Surely this alone would be enough to provoke scientific inquiry into the nature of water. In fact, science itself has recently added its own vast body of discoveries about water and its centrality to the life of this planet.

It should now become clear that the scientific and the spiritual qualities are simply two sides of the same coin. So, for example, just as water can store memories and be influenced by thoughts and feelings, so it's also able to use this absorptive property to remove and cleanse negative emotions and their effects from people and leave them prepared to move on in their lives. This is an aspect widely used in religion; the indigenous cultures of South America use waterfalls to this end, while the Hindus of India bathe in their sacred rivers, especially the Ganges.

We can hope that in time, all modern societies will come to honor water and its spirit as much as ancient traditions have done through the ages. That's certainly my desire and intention.

CHAPTER 11

WATER IN CHRISTIANITY

by Alan Walker

The Bible begins and ends with images of water. At the beginning of creation, "darkness was upon the face of the deep, and the spirit of God moved upon the face of the waters" (Genesis 1:2). At the end of time there will be a new heaven and new Earth. There will be no more sea, but "a pure river of water of life, clear as a crystal" (Revelation 22:1) will flow from God and quench the thirst of all who drink from it (Revelation 22:17).

In the mythological worldview of the Old Testament, water stands for the primeval chaos that God must overcome to begin His work of creation. The sky (or "heaven") is a "dome" in the midst of the waters, separating the ones above from those below (Genesis 1:6–8). Then the waters below are gathered together in one place so that dry land might appear, and so the sea and the earth are created (Genesis 1:9–10).

We hear echoes elsewhere in the Hebrew scriptures of a primordial battle between God and sea monsters: "You divided the sea by your might; you broke the heads of the dragons of the waters. You crushed the head of Leviathan" (Psalm 74:13–14).

God's work of creation, therefore, hasn't destroyed the primeval chaos, but pushed it back. The sea is set limits, and the waters are ordered to stick to them (Proverbs 8:29); but they still pose a threat. Humans are aware that their lives are, as it were, suspended over the brink. Not surprisingly, the biblical writers looked forward to a time when this threat would be removed—when "God will punish Leviathan the fleeing serpent, Leviathan the twisting serpent, and he will slay the dragon that is in the sea" (Isaiah 27:1)—and saw a dry ocean as a sign of the final establishment of God's rule on Earth.

In the meantime, God keeps the waters under control so that those "who went down to the sea in ships, doing business on the mighty waters . . . saw the deeds of the Lord, his wondrous works in the deep" (Psalm 107:23–4).

When God despairs of the wickedness of humankind and resolves to undo His creation, He does so by unleashing the waters in a flood, allowing only Noah and his family to survive (Genesis 6–7). Later, when the Israelites are escaping from Egypt, God separates the waters of the Red Sea to allow them to cross and releases them to destroy the Egyptians (Exodus 14–15).

Of course, for the most part, water appears in the ordinary sense of the word in the Old Testament as an essential element for drinking and washing, particularly so for a people living in or on the edge of a desert. Paradise was portrayed as an oasis, and water was also used to depict the blessings that came from God: "Let justice roll down like waters, and righteousness like an ever-flowing stream" (Amos 5:24).

In the New Testament, Jesus begins his ministry in the wilderness of Judea by being baptized by John in the river Jordan (Matthew 3). *Baptism* originally simply meant to "dip" or "immerse" in water. In the 1st century, the Jews had a ceremony of "proselyte baptism," which was an initiation ritual for converts to Judaism. John says his baptism is "for repentance" (Matthew 3:11), and he understands it as preparation for an imminent fresh intervention by God in the world.

Christians believe that moment arrived with the Incarnation— the entry of the Son, the second person of the Trinity, into the world as a man. By sharing our human nature, God makes it possible for us to "participate in the divine nature" (2 Peter 1:4). By dying and rising again, Jesus Christ conquers death and offers a share in his risen life to all who identify with him through faith and are baptized.

Christian baptism, therefore, has a much broader and more profound meaning than that of John. It's not simply a ceremony marking entry into the Christian community in the way that circumcision marks a boy's membership to the Jewish people, and it's far more than a "naming" ceremony.

Baptism is a mystical participation in the death and resurrection of Christ. The candidate goes under the water, "drowning" to his or her old life, and is then dramatically drawn out into a new kind of existence. Christians believe that the church isn't simply an association of like-minded people, but is the very "body of Christ," which, in another mode, burst out of the tomb at Easter. In the early church, baptisms were principally conducted at Easter to reinforce this connection.

In the baptismal liturgy, the water is blessed with words that call attention to the place of water in the history of salvation:

> Father, we give you thanks and praise for your gift of water in creation; for your Spirit, sweeping over the waters, bringing light and life.
>
> You delivered Noah from the waters of destruction; you divided the waters of the sea, and by the hand of Moses you led your people from slavery into the Promised Land.
>
> In water your son Jesus received the baptism of John. . . . In it we are buried with Christ in his death. By it we share in his resurrection.
>
> May your holy and life-giving Spirit move upon these waters. Restore through them the beauty of your creation. . . . Drown sin in the waters of judgement.
>
> Now sanctify this water that . . . they may be cleansed from sin and born again. . . . (*Common Worship: Christian Initiation,* 2006)

The meaning of baptism as a "drowning," clear when performed as an immersion, has been obscured by the practice of baptism by "affusion" (pouring) or "aspersion" (sprinkling) and by the use of bowl-like fonts. Similarly, this has also encouraged a misplaced emphasis on the aspect of "cleansing" in baptism, which is confusing (even distressing) when the candidate is an infant.

Christians understand baptism to be a washing away of "original sin," the condition of being alienated from God, which is characteristic of all humanity and mythologically inherited from their first parents, Adam and Eve. This is possible precisely because the human Christ has paid the penalty for sin in his death on the cross and made possible again the fellowship humanity enjoyed with God in the Garden of Eden.

Baptism is described in Christian theology as a *sacrament,* that is to say, "an outward and visible sign of an inward and spiritual grace" *(Book of Common Prayer)*. It's an "effective" sign, one that actually brings about what it signifies, by which God works invisibly within us.

Sacraments are not magical. They're not at the disposal of men and women who happen to know the words or how to perform the actions. They work because part of humanity is being restored to its proper relationship with God, and so to its intended dignity and status. They belong to a redeemed space within the "fallen" world.

In the language of the gospels, this space was called the "kingdom" of God and was actualized when Christ lived on Earth and "went about among us." The miracles that he performed may be interpreted as signs of the kingdom "overflowing" into mundane reality. Interestingly, the first of these was the transformation of water into wine at the wedding feast in Cana (John 2:1–11).

Wine itself is, of course, pregnant with meaning in Christianity. At the Last Supper, Jesus identifies wine with his own blood and instructs his disciples to share wine in memory of him until they're reunited in heaven (Matthew 26:26–29). The next day, Good Friday, they see blood and water flowing from his side when it's pierced by a Roman soldier's spear to confirm that he has truly died on the cross (John 19:34).

To this day, when Christians meet to remember Jesus, a little water is mingled with the wine that is to "become" his blood. As the priest does this, he whispers one of the "secret" prayers: "By the mystery of this water and wine, may we share the divinity of Christ as he humbled himself to share our humanity." The wine represents the divinity, the water the humanity. In the Eucharist— the mystic supper—Christians have a foretaste of the divine life that's promised to them and prefigured in the turning of water into wine at the marriage feast.

We're to understand the occasion when Jesus "walks on water" (Matthew 14:22–33) in a similar way. The miracle is not a display of power in which Jesus bypasses the laws of nature, nor is it a "natural" act that the eyewitnesses failed to understand (such as that Jesus was actually walking on submerged ice). What the disciples are witnessing is a manifestation of the world as it's meant to be and was before the Fall, a world where the forces of nature and humanity are in harmony with one another. Jesus even encourages Peter to follow him onto the sea as a foretaste of the restored creation.

There are other occasions in the gospels in which water plays a central role and illuminates important aspects of Christian teaching. At Jacob's Well, Jesus asks a Samaritan woman who's drawing water if she could give him a drink. When she expresses surprise for "religious" reasons (Jews normally had no dealings with Samaritans), Jesus tells her that if she'd known who he was, she would have asked *him* for a drink and would have received in return "living water": "Everyone who drinks of this [well] water will be thirsty again, but those who drink of the water that I will give them will never be thirsty" (John 4:13–14).

He isn't simply using a metaphor in which water represents faith. Jesus is pointing to a time when the elements, along with the whole of creation, will be restored. Christianity doesn't reject the material world or consider it as in opposition to the spiritual. Everything God made is "good" (Genesis 1:31); although everything, too, has been affected by humanity's disobedience.

At the Last Supper, Jesus "poured water into a basin and began to wash the disciples' feet" (John 13:5). He tells them, "Unless I wash you, you have no share in me" (John 13:8), thus making a connection with baptism. The next day, his life will be poured out like water on their behalf. Then he instructs them to "wash one another's feet" (John 13:14) because "sharing" in him isn't an individual but a social experience. Salvation in Christian terms isn't an escape from the world, but a call to the service of others. A ceremony of the washing of feet is performed each year in Christian churches at the beginning of the Maundy Thursday liturgy. In England, it was for centuries the custom of the monarch to wash the feet of some poor people on that occasion and to give them a small gift of money. Today the Queen still gives gifts of "Maundy money."

In the early centuries of the church beyond the New Testament period, water came to play an important role in worship and devotion. The theological rationale for "holy water" was that as Jesus had been sinless and in no need of "washing," his presence in the Jordan had the effect of sanctifying the water. The water of the Jordan is today considered by many Christians to have a sacred character, and bottles of it are sought after. Members of the English royal family have been baptized in Jordan water since the time of the Crusades.

There's evidence that water was blessed in Egypt in the 3rd century for use in exorcisms and in curing illness, and since the 4th century it has been the custom in the Eastern churches to bless water on the feast of the Epiphany in memory of Jesus' baptism by John. This water is made available to members of the church to bless their homes and possessions and to drink in time of illness or special need. On one of the following days, a visit is made to bless the sea or a nearby river or lake as a sign of the redemption of all creation through Christ. Sometimes a wooden cross is placed in the water. A blessing of the Thames from Southwark Bridge has been revived in recent years by Anglicans in London.

In the West, holy water is first recorded as being used in the 6th century for the dedication of a church. This water was mixed with wine, salt, and ashes.

Today, holy water is often found in a stoup at the entrance to churches for the faithful to dip a finger in before making the sign of the cross. It's used to sprinkle the congregation at the beginning of the principal Sunday service or on other occasions as a reminder of their baptism. During the year, the harvest gifts or the Christmas tree, for example, are sprinkled to "set them apart" from ordinary use; and any appropriate object or place may be blessed in the same way.

In Christianity, neither places nor the natural elements are endowed with any intrinsic supernatural or spiritual power, but because of the Christian belief in the inherent goodness of creation, any natural source of water has the potential to be considered holy "by association."

One of the best-known examples is Lourdes in France, where the Virgin Mary appeared to Bernadette Soubirous in 1858 and instructed her to uncover a spring, which would have healing properties [see Chapter 16]. Another is the Holy Well at Walsingham in England, where a spring of water gushed up at the site of the Virgin Mary's appearance to Richeldis de Faverches, the lady of the manor, in 1061. Today pilgrims receive the water there in three ways: as a drink (for the health of the body), with the sign of the cross (for the soul), and in the cupped hands (for the spirit).

Nevertheless, because God is not only a transcendent reality beyond the world He has made but also an immanent reality active within it, many Christians would accept that a variety of times, places, and materials have the potentiality of revealing the mystery of God. However, they'd always affirm that in any encounter, it's God Who takes the initiative. He's never at our disposal; He's always a God of surprises.

CHAPTER 12

MIKVAH: GATEWAY TO PURITY

by Rivkah Slonim

In the beginning, there was only water. A miraculous compound, it's the vivifying force of all life as we know it. But it is more. For these very same attributes—water as source and sustaining energy—are mirrored in the spiritual. Water has the power to purify, restore, and replenish life to our essential spiritual selves.

Jewish tradition relates that after being banished from Eden, Adam sat in a river that flowed from the garden as part of his attempt to return to his original perfection. To this day, water in a *mikvah* pool is used as a means of purification.

The world's natural bodies of water—its oceans, wells, and spring-fed lakes—are mikvahs in their most primal form. They contain waters of Divine source and thus, Jewish tradition teaches, the power to purify. Created even before the world took shape, these bodies of water offer a quintessential route to consecration. However, they may be inaccessible or dangerous, and there may be additional problems of inclement weather and lack of privacy. Jewish life therefore necessitates the construction of mikvah pools, and indeed this has been done by Jews of every age and circumstance.

To the uninitiated, a modern-day mikvah looks very much like a miniature swimming pool. Its ordinary appearance, however, belies the complex web of laws that surround its construction and its primary place in Jewish life and law. The mikvah offers the individual, the community, and the nation of Israel the remarkable gift of purity and holiness. No other religious structure or rite can affect the Jew in this way and on such an essential level.

The mikvah's extraordinary power has held sway since the dawn of time. Before the revelation at Sinai, all Jews were commanded to immerse themselves in preparation for coming face to face with God. In the desert, the famed well of Miriam served as a mikvah, and Aaron and his sons' induction into the priesthood was marked by immersion in it. In Temple times, the priests and any other Jew who wished to enter the House of God had to first immerse themselves in a mikvah. On Yom Kippur, the Jewish day of atonement and most sacred of all days, the high priest was allowed entrance into the Holy of Holies, the innermost chamber of the Temple, which no other mortal could enter. This was the zenith of a day that involved an ascending order of services, each of which was preceded by immersion in the mikvah.

The primary uses of the mikvah today date back to the dawn of Jewish history and cover many elements of Jewish life. The most important and general usage is for purification by the menstruating woman within a framework known as *taharat hamishpachah,* family purity. Briefly, from the onset of a woman's menses until after immersion in a mikvah, which takes place seven days after the cessation of her menses, the woman and husband are prohibited from expressing their love for each other in a physical manner.

The observance of family purity and immersion in the mikvah within that framework is a biblical injunction of the highest order. While most see the synagogue as the central institution in Jewish life, Jewish law states that constructing a mikvah takes precedence over building a house of worship. Jewish married life, and therefore the birth of future generations in accordance with Jewish law, is possible only where there is access to a mikvah. It's clearly no exaggeration to state that the mikvah is the touchstone of Jewish life and the portal to a Jewish future.

In primitive societies, menstruating women were a source of consternation and fear. Peace could be made with menstruation only by ascribing it to evil and demonic spirits and by the adaptation of a social structure that facilitated its avoidance. Viewed against this backdrop, the Jewish rhythm in marriage is perceived by many as a throwback to archaic taboos, a system rooted in antiquated attitudes and a ubiquitous form of misogyny. In truth, family purity is a celebration of life and our most precious human relationships. It can be understood most fully within the larger concept of ritual purity and impurity.

Judaism teaches that the source of all *taharah*, "purity," is life itself. Conversely, death is the harbinger of *tumah*, "impurity." All types of ritual impurity—and the Bible describes many—are rooted in the absence of life or some measure—even a whisper—of death.

When stripped to its essence, a woman's menses signals the death of potential life. Each month, a woman's body prepares for the possibility of conception. The uterine lining is built up rich and replete, ready to serve as a cradle for life in anticipation of a fertilized ovum. Menstruation is the shedding of the lining, the end of this possibility. The presence of potential life within fills a woman's body with holiness and purity. With the departure of this potential, impurity sets in, conferring upon the woman a state of impurity or, more specifically, *niddut*. Impurity is neither evil nor dangerous, and it isn't something tangible. It's a spiritual state of being, the absence of purity, much as darkness is the absence of light. Only immersion in the mikvah, following the requisite preparation, can change it.

The concept of purity and impurity as mandated by the Bible and applied within Jewish life is unique. It's often difficult for the contemporary mind to relate to the notion and view it as relevant. In ancient times, however, *tumah* and *taharah* were central and determining factors. The status of a Jew, whether ritually pure or impure, was at the very core of Jewish living. It dictated and regulated a person's involvement in all areas of ritual. Most notably, *tumah* made entrance into the Holy Temple impossible.

There were numerous types of impurities that affected Jews, regarding both their life and Temple service, and a commensurate number of purification processes; but mikvah immersion was the culmination of the purification rite in every case. Even for the ritually pure, ascending to a higher level of spiritual involvement or holiness necessitated immersion in a mikvah. As such, the institution of mikvah took center stage in Jewish life.

In this post-Temple period, the power and interplay of ritual status has all but vanished, relegating this dynamic to obscurity.

There is, however, one arena in which purity and impurity continue to be pivotal. In this connection only does there continue to be a biblical mandate for mikvah immersion—and that's regarding human sexuality. Lovemaking signals the possibility and potential for new life, the formation of a new body, and the descent from heaven of a new soul. In their fusing, man and woman become part of something larger; in their transcendence of the self, they draw on, and even touch, the Divine. They enter into a partnership with God; they come closest to taking on the Godly attribute of creator. In fact, the sacredness of the intimate union remains unmitigated even when the possibility of conception doesn't exist. In the metaphysical sense, the act and its potential remain linked.

Human sexuality is a primary force in the lives of a married couple; it's the unique language and expression of the love they share. A strong relationship between husband and wife is not only the backbone of their own family unit, but is integral to the world at large. The blessings of trust, stability, continuity, and, ultimately, community all flow from the commitment they have to each other and to a joint future. In reaffirming their commitment in their intimacy, the couple adds to the vibrancy and health of their society and to the fruition of the Divine plan: a world perfected by humans. As such, they're engaged in the most sacred of pursuits.

In this light, it becomes clear why marital relations are often referred to as the holy temple of human endeavor. And entrance to the holy always was, and continues to be, contingent on ritual purity. Immersion in the mikvah is the gateway to the holy ground of conjugality.

There are other important usages of the mikvah as well. Mikvah is an integral part of conversion to Judaism. New pots, dishes, and utensils must be immersed in a mikvah before they may be used. The mikvah concept is also the focal point of the purification rite of a Jew before being laid to eternal rest and the soul ascending on high. Finally, Jewish men also use the mikvah on various occasions for the purpose of heightened purification. With the exception of conversion, however, these uses are all customary.

Immersion in a mikvah effects a change in status; more correctly, an elevation in status. Utensils that could heretofore not be used can, after immersion, be utilized in the holy act of eating as a Jew. A woman who from the onset of her menses was in a state of *niddut,* abstaining from sexual relations with her husband, may be reunited with him after immersion in the ultimate holiness of married intimacy. Men or women in Temple times, who were precluded from services because of ritual defilement, could, after immersion, enter the House of God. The case of the convert is most dramatic. The individual who descends into the mikvah as a Gentile emerges from beneath its waters as a Jew.

So the mikvah personifies both the womb and the grave, the portals to life and the afterlife. In both, the person is stripped of all power and prowess. In both there's a mode of total reliance, complete abdication of control.

Immersion in the mikvah can be understood as a symbolic act of self-abnegation, the conscious suspension of the self as an autonomous force. The person immersing signals a desire to achieve oneness with the Source of all life, God. Immersion indicates the abandonment of one form of existence to embrace one infinitely higher. It's thus described not only in terms of purification, revitalization, and rejuvenation, but also—perhaps primarily—as rebirth.

○ ○ ○

RESOURCES

Aryeh Kaplan, *Waters of Eden: The Mystery of the Mikvah,* Union of Orthodox Jewish Congregations of Ame, 1993.

Rivkah Slonim, *Total Immersion: A Mikvah Anthology,* Jason Aronson, 1996.

Deena R. Zimmerman, *A Lifetime Companion to the Laws of Jewish Family Life,* Urim Publications, 2005.

www.mikvah.org

www.yoatzot.org

○ ○ ○   ○ ○ ○

CHAPTER 13

WATERS OF THE WORLD

by Starhawk

O ne morning I was meditating beside a beautiful lake in Vermont, listening for whatever messages the water might have for me. "All water is connected," the lake said. "All water is in constant communication with all other water. The waters of the world are one—one consciousness, holding the world in liquid embrace. What you do to any part of the waters affects them all."

I am a Pagan, someone who practices the ancient Earth-based religions that have roots in pre-Christian traditions of Europe and the Middle East. For Pagans, water is one of the four sacred elements—earth, air, fire, and water—with the fifth, the spirit, honored as the center of the sacred circle. These things are revered because they're the basis of life. We begin every ritual by honoring and invoking them, and end every ceremony by thanking them and bidding them good-bye, reminding ourselves again and again of our deep dependence on the natural world.

To say that water is sacred has both spiritual and practical implications. If we honor water spiritually, we must also treat it with respect in very ordinary ways. The land I live on, in the coastal mountains of western Sonoma County, California, is a place of water extremes. In the winter, we can get 80 to 100 inches of rain, which often comes in torrents. Hillsides wash away, and nearby rivers flood. We learn to respect water's power to carve, to change, to undermine, and to rage—and we know that every structure we build, every road we lay, and every bridge and crossing we construct must be designed to respect and channel water's flow, or we risk immense damage to the land.

The salmon and steelhead trout, keystone species of these hills, depend on clean gravel in running streams and deep summer pools in order to reproduce. The health of the hills and forests, in turn, depends on the salmon, who, as they migrate back from the sea and swim upriver to their birth streams to spawn and die, return nutrients that have washed downstream to the soil and the trees. But a century and a half of logging, gravel mining, and road building has silted much of the gravel and dried up the summer pools. To hold water sacred, we must cherish the salmon and work to repair the damage.

Water also teaches us to be *humble*—a word that shares a root with "humus" and means "close to the earth." For our greatest allies in cleansing and healing water are the most humble things on Earth—bacteria, fungi, beneficial microbes, and plants. Gray-water systems provide habitat for these creatures, who obligingly eat pathogens. Sewage can be treated in constructed wetlands or "living machines" that mimic nature's own ways of cleansing water, sending it through a sequence of living communities of bacteria, algae, plants, and fish.[1]

Conserving water and creating systems to heal and clean it are practical prayers. We've also created rituals that honor water's powers of cleansing and connecting. For many years, Reclaiming, my extended spiritual community, has practiced a simple ritual we call "Waters of the World." We collect water—from sacred springs and from our household taps, from significant places and from the sites of significant events—and combine it when we come together in ritual, often keeping a bowl of it on the altar so that it becomes infused with our energy. Then, when we separate, we each take a small amount. Some of us carry it with us wherever we go, using it to make offerings to the earth and to give back to the spirits of any place where we collect more water.

This ritual began more than two decades ago as a response to fear and despair. It was in 1980, shortly after Ronald Reagan was elected President of the United States, when our circle met for the winter solstice. We held an all-night vigil and spoke about

our deep fear that the new regime would undermine hard-won environmental protections and might even lead us into nuclear war. We decided to hold a larger ritual on February Eve, the feast of Brigid, who is the ancient Celtic goddess of the holy well and sacred flame and presides over smithcraft, poetry, and healing.

We began with a simple cleansing ritual. We divided the gathering of about 100 people into small groups and gave each a bowl of salt water. We asked the groups to pass the bowls counterclockwise—the direction of banishing and releasing—giving each person a chance to speak about the places in their lives where they felt powerless and to imagine the feelings as a muddy stream flowing into the bowls. Then we sang, chanted, and poured our spiritual energy into the bowls to transform the energy locked up in hopelessness and despair. Salt—a crystal—helps bind and focus energy.

When we could see the bowls glowing with light and feel the energy shifting, we passed the bowls clockwise, letting each person dip their fingers into the water to take back some of the transformed energy and speak about where in their lives they felt power, love, and hope.

This water-cleansing ritual is one I've often used in personal meditation when my thoughts and emotions were churning with anger or stress. I've used it in groups, placing a bowl of salt water in the center of a group in conflict and asking people to speak their frustrations and bitterness into the bowl, then raising power to cleanse and transform the energy so that it can be taken back. In all these rituals we focus on honoring the energy locked up in anger or grief or resentment, seeing it not as something negative to be gotten rid of, but as something potentially strong, powerful, and positive that has gotten stuck and stagnant and needs to be released to flow more freely.

That first despair ritual led us into action to stop the building of an unsafe nuclear power plant and protest the development and testing of nuclear weapons. Brigid's feast became a time for us to do rituals to strengthen our commitment to act in the world to protect what was sacred to us: the elements that sustain life; the human and plant and animal communities that depend on them; and those real but intangible qualities—freedom, justice, compassion, and love—that infuse life with spirit.

One year, we decided to create Brigid's well—a big punch bowl filled with waters from special places. My friend Luisah Teish is a Yoruba Priestess of Oshun, the river *orisha,* or "spirit power." When I was traveling once, I asked Teish what I could bring back for her, and she said, "Water." So I began collecting water from special places, and that gave us the idea to create the well. We added water from many places that were important to us, from sacred springs and wells and from our homes, and saved some back at the end of the ritual. Now, more than two decades later, our Waters of the World contain water from every continent and ocean, even from Antarctica, from sacred rivers and Brigid's well and from the many political actions we've done to save and preserve water. They're a living embodiment of the message I heard from the lake—that all water is one.

In recent years, the issue of protecting water has become a central one for me and many of my friends. In today's world, water is seen as a commodity to be bought, sold, privatized, and hoarded for profit. More than a billion people lack access to safe drinking water.

> "Tell me about your home. . . . Who owns the water?"
> "Nobody owns it. You can't own water, where I come from."
> "Somebody's got to own it. . . . Somebody always does."
> "We believe there are Four Sacred Things that can't be owned . . .
> water is one of them . . . because they belong to everybody.
> Because everybody's life depends on them."
> "But that would make them the best kind of thing to own. . . ."[2]

That scrap of dialogue from my 1993 novel, *The Fifth Sacred Thing,* expresses the heart of the conflict. It's estimated that the resource wars of the 21st century will center on water. If we hold water sacred, if we want to preserve it as a source of peace, fertility, and life—not a ground for conflict—we must be active in establishing and protecting access to it as a human right.

With a loose group of spiritually based activists that we call the Pagan Cluster, I've many times taken part in demonstrations and protests to protect water rights. We dress in blue and carry puppets or rivers of cloth suspended on sticks to represent a Living River. In April 2001, we took part in demonstrations against the Free Trade Area of the Americas, an international trade agreement that would have privatized water across three continents. We danced and chanted through a haze of tear gas, bringing the free spirit of water to the gates of power, along with the Cochabamba Declaration, written by the people of that Bolivian city who in January of 2000 took back their water supply from privatization by rebelling, filling the streets, and shutting down the city for two weeks until the government relented. Their eloquent and poetic statement became, for us, a sacred document:

THE COCHABAMBA DECLARATION

For the right to life, for the respect of nature and the uses and traditions of our ancestors and our peoples, for all time the following shall be declared as inviolable rights with regard to the uses of water given us by the earth:

1. Water belongs to the earth and all species and is sacred to life, therefore the world's water must be conserved, reclaimed and protected for all future generations and its natural patterns respected.

2. Water is a fundamental human right and a public trust to be guarded by all levels of government, therefore it should not be commodified, privatized or traded for commercial purposes. These rights must be enshrined at all levels of government. In particular, an international treaty must ensure these principles are noncontrovertible.

3. Water is best protected by local communities and citizens who must be respected as equal partners with governments in the protection and regulation of water.

Peoples of the earth are the only vehicle to promote earth democracy and save water.[3]

All water is one. Whenever we're working to protect, heal, and respect water in practical ways and advocating the rights of every human being to clean water, or honoring water through ritual and ceremony and connecting with its deep spiritual healing and cleansing powers, we're acknowledging and celebrating the deep unifying life force that sustains us. Our practical and political efforts give our prayers strength and integrity; our prayers and rituals sustain our spirits for the hard work of service, healing, and action.

☼ ☼ ☼

NOTES

1. See John Todd's work on living machines: **www.oceanarks.org**

2. Starhawk, *The Fifth Sacred Thing*, NY: Bantam, 1993: pp.71–2.

3. The Cochabamba Declaration can be found at: **www.starhawk.org/activism/cochabamba-dec.html** and **www.nadir.org/nadir/initiativ/agp/free/imf/bolivia/cochabamba.htm**

For an account of the uprising, see "Bolivia's War over Water" by Jim Schultz, at **www.democracyctr.org/waterwar**

FURTHER INFORMATION

Starhawk's Website: **www.starhawk.org**

To receive her periodic writings and schedule, e-mail **Starhawk-subscribe@lists.riseup.net**

For more information on Starhawk's Earth Activist Trainings, see: **www.earthactivisttraining.org**

☼ ☼ ☼   ☼ ☼ ☼

CHAPTER 14

THE SPIRIT OF WATER
IN THE WORLD OF SHAMANISM

by José Luis Stevens, Ph.D.

INTRODUCTION

In the course of my life, I've been most fortunate to study and work closely with elders and men and women of knowledge from several shamanically oriented tribal cultures. I've witnessed extraordinary healings and methods of communicating with the elements that radically challenged my university-bred beliefs about the nature of reality and gave me insight into the possibilities that I'd been trained to screen out by my traditional Western education. In particular, I've observed what a unique and central place the element of water has in the teachings and beliefs of these extraordinary peoples.

In this article, I'll focus on three tribes with a shamanic base from diverse locations in the world, yet ones that well represent the universal shamanic understandings about the nature of water and its properties. First, I'll present a simple introduction to shamanism and then a description of the Shipibo culture from the Peruvian Amazon and the centrality of water in their world. Next, I'll look at the Huichol tribe from rugged central Mexico and examine some of their most profound insights into the nature of the spirit of water. Finally, I'll compare this with how the Tuvan people from Mongolia understand and relate to water in their traditional shamanic culture.

A BRIEF EXPLANATION OF ANIMISM AND SHAMANISM

Animism is the world's most ancient set of spiritual beliefs regarding the nature of reality and is now seeing an upswing of interest in every continent. Its premise is that everything in the universe is alive and highly conscious and has a uniquely intelligent soul.

Animism is based on the belief that the world consists of overlapping energy fields and that underlying the visible world is the spirit world, the origin of all power, energy, and vitality. Consequently, animists believe that invisible forces or spirits can affect physical elements such as water, fire, air, earth, plants, animals, and people. Animistic cultures believe in showing the utmost respect to the spirits in everything—whether they be clouds rocks, winds, springs, or birds of prey—as all are participants in the greater community of life.

While animism refers to the beliefs of the members of a tribe or community at large, shamanism is a specialty developed within that society by certain individuals. It requires acquired skills, knowledge, and natural talents. However, it's not a religion because it has no structured hierarchy or set of dogmas; rather, it's a set of special techniques for manipulating energy and power.

Shamans specialize in diagnosing and healing illness and suffering, divining and prophesying, journeying to other worlds through trance states to seek knowledge to gain control over spirits, and gathering and storing power through techniques and practices associated with nature. They're known to make special use of trance to manipulate and control the weather, speak with the spirits of plants and animals, and conduct strenuous ceremonies for fertility, healing, and sorcery. Without the ancient practice of shamanism, it's unlikely that humans would have survived prehistoric times, as it includes many practical techniques designed to solve everyday problems and to aid survival in the world's harshest environments.

The word *shaman* comes from the language of the Tungus people in Siberia and was initially used by anthropologists to describe the unique practices and experiences of shamans in that culture. Today the term has grown in popular usage to include similar customs in cultures all over the world.

The practice of shamanism is remarkably similar from continent to continent, even though in many cases there has been little or no contact between the shamans of the Amazon, the Andes, the steppes of Asia, Africa, Australia, Europe, Polynesia, and all of North America. Shamans from all over the planet say that this similarity is a result of their cross-cultural use of deep trance to access the *axis mundi,* the universal tree of life, an invisible highway leading to all locations in the world.

Common to all shamanic cultures and peoples is the central importance of the spirit of water, for without it there would be no plants and animals, and it's from these that shamans learn some of their most cherished secrets. It's through their alliance with these totems that they gather much of their power to create, manipulate, and thus control reality.

THE RELATIONSHIP OF THE SHIPIBO TO WATER

The Conibo-Shipibo are a combined tribe of approximately 30,000 people living in the Peruvian Amazon around the Ucayali river system, one of the two main sources of the Amazon. Theirs is truly a world of water; and from it they derive their primary food staples, the fish and many of the plants they rely on for survival. Their lifestyle and beliefs are typical of many of the varied tribes in the Amazon region. However, they're considered the ones with the greatest knowledge of shamanic practices, and therefore many shamans of other tribes study with them to learn their potent sorceric skills, as well as their powerful *icaros,* sacred songs for healing and controlling the elements. For the last 15 years, my wife, Lena, and I have been traveling to their jungle homeland to study and train with the Shipibo elders Doña Juana, Don Carlos, and Don Niko; and from them and their families we've gained some understanding of the importance of water in their cosmology and how they interact with it in ceremony and healing.

According to them, the Shipibo (for short), a shamanically based culture, believe that Roni, the giant anaconda, created the world using the pattern on its back to manifest the patterns in all the forms of reality, including the human body, the land, the sky, the waters, and all the plants and animals. Roni makes its home in the rivers of the Amazon, the lifeblood and transportation system for all jungle tribes in this region of the world. The Shipibo are most grateful to Roni for providing this grand-patterned landscape, and thus they focus on discerning the energetic designs in everything around them through the traditional use of *ayahuasca,* a mixture of plants that when cooked and taken in ceremony produces powerful insights and visions regarding the vibrating subatomic structures of the elements, the plants, and the animals. For thousands of years, through their ancestral use of ayahuasca, they've seen and learned the intricate patterns and the songs woven into every aspect of life. This gives them the power to communicate with, learn from, and command the powers of everything around them—including the powerful spirit of water.

I've seen how they reproduce these beautiful patterns on textiles, on the walls of their buildings, and even on their skin in the form of vegetable-dyed tattoos for protection, healing, and gaining knowledge. Among the countless specific designs they reproduce are the patterns for the sun, the earth, the plants, and of course the spirit of the water. In healing practices, they specifically use the patterns of the water to purify and cleanse the body of unwanted foreign intrusions.

According to Don Carlos, the Shipibo believe that each object has its original pattern and that these patterns can in turn carry others within them. The pattern for water is especially capable of carrying other designs in a way that's similar to a boat transporting people or cargo. He tells me that since the human body consists mostly of water, it's a strong vehicle for carrying other patterns, sometimes positive ones and at times negative. The negative patterns, resulting from other people's fearful or angry thoughts and from plants and animals that have been disrespected, can throw the physical or emotional body out of balance and thus create illness, depression, or other

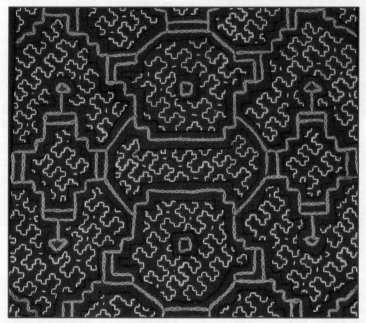

Song for the power of water

Song of the water spirits for protection

disharmonious states. These alien patterns can be extracted and replaced with the positive songs representing the designs of beneficial plants, animals, and elements.

The patterns for water and its infinite variations are also used to promote prosperity and abundance for individuals who are having trouble manifesting what they want in their life. This pattern may be tattooed on their skin, using temporary plant dyes, or placed around their shoulders in the form of an embroidered shawl. It might even be worn as an article of clothing, such as a skirt; and it could be painted on the side of their boat.

Variations of the pattern for water may involve the design for a good catch while fishing; for learning from the powerful spirits of the river dolphins; for protection from Roni the water anaconda; and the motifs for springs, waterfalls, pools, rain, clouds, and rainbows.

For the Shipibo, as with most shamanic cultures, water is considered a great power, a *poderio,* a force that embodies spirits that may be helpful or harmful. Reproducing its patterns and the designs, then, is a way of showing respect for them and harnessing the power inherent within them. For example, by wearing the design for the spirit of the river, someone might then navigate safely upon it and fish from it with success. In other words, the Shipibo have learned to become that with which they wish to be in harmony.

According to Don Niko, mermaids and dolphins are particularly powerful water spirits that can be asked for help in a variety of situations. He says that the ancient shamans used to dive into the river and commune with these spirits, learning songs from them and gathering the wisdom they chose to share. He says that today this is mostly a lost art and that therefore these water spirits create problems because people no longer show them honor or respect.

Nevertheless, during ayahuasca ceremonies, it's not unusual for the participants to experience the spirit of the river coursing through the veins and organs of the body, washing, cleaning, purifying, and protecting. The result is a roaring sensation or a rushing sound of water in the ears that may last for hours.

During one such ceremony in the jungle, my visions enabled me to meet the loving spirit of a specific river in the Amazon. It told me that we had met very long ago and that it had been my totem many times before. This spirit told me its name and explained that it had been with me all my life and had taught me many things while protecting me from dangers. I suddenly recalled the many years I had been a river rafter safely navigating the rapids in the Grand Canyon and in many difficult rivers in California, Colorado, Idaho, and Alaska. I recalled a song that I'd spontaneously begun to sing about the river being my friend during a rafting trip down the Salmon River in Idaho many years prior. This brought tears to my eyes, and I realized that this river spirit was indeed my old friend and that I owed it respect for its protection and assistance. The river spirit told me that I could call upon it anytime by experiencing it coursing through my body, and it would help me in any way it could as long as I told it what I wanted.

On another occasion I went for a walk in the jungle with a friend. We found a big pool with a waterfall pouring into it, and we both stood underneath the falls—I briefly, but he for a long while. Later that day, he wasn't feeling too well. That night in ceremony I overheard the *ayahuasquero* (shaman conducting the ceremony) explain to my friend that he'd stood under a waterfall for too long and had taken on too much of its spirit, and that was why he was feeling sick. The shaman explained that the spirit was benevolent but that my friend had simply absorbed an excess of it in his body. He performed an extraction, sucking out the excess of the pattern for that water spirit, and my friend's health was restored. I was truly amazed that the shaman had been able to detect exactly what had happened, given that we hadn't told him about the incident.

During healing ceremonies, I've witnessed Doña Juana and many of her fellow Shipibo healers filling small basins with a little bit of water, which they then cast extractions into, often by spitting or vomiting foreign objects into the bowls. They then visually study the extractions floating in the water in order to diagnose the problem. Afterward, they toss the water away. They see the water as a great cleanser and purifier, and never is a healing ceremony conducted without its benevolent presence.

On numerous occasions I've seen the Shipibo healers sing icaros (those sacred songs derived from the patterns of nature) into a glass or bottle of plain water, and the patient is then instructed to drink a little of the water all day long or over a period of days. Again, the understanding is that water is a medium in which prayers and songs can be held and then carried into the patient's original healthy pattern. The water itself has its own structured design, but may also carry additional patterns sung into it, designs that are beneficial to the recipient.

For the Shipibo, all forms of water are powers to learn from and work with. Doña Juana is an elder Shipibo woman with great knowledge of the icaros passed down to her through generations of ancestors. She tells me that her greatest ally is the spirit of rain, which she can call forth with her icaros to purify and cleanse the land. I've heard her sing an icaro for rain and bring in a thunderstorm within a half hour. Such practices aren't by any means exclusive to the Shipibo people, of course, but are to be found all over the Amazon and, for that matter, anywhere shamans use their skills. Having water as an ally in its varied forms is part and parcel of shamanic practice everywhere.

THE HUICHOLS'S RELATIONSHIP TO WATER

Let's now shift our focus from the Shipibo people and move it north to Central Mexico to become acquainted with the powerful Huichol people and their understanding of the power of water. The Huichols live in the states of Jalisco and Nayarit, in a harsh mountain range stretching from the interior of Mexico to the Pacific Ocean. Numbering about 20,000, they are one of two tribes in Mexico who've managed to preserve their original culture from destruction at the hands of the Spanish invasion. They have strong shamanic roots with a rich tradition of collecting peyote, which they ingest during multiple day and night ceremonies and rituals.

The Huichols, like all shamanic cultures, honor the spirits of nature and call upon them during healing and fertility ceremonies. Fundamental to their cosmology is the Pacific Ocean, one of their primary *poderios,* the great powers they work with.

They call the spirit of the sea *Tatei Haramara*—*Tatei* for "our Mother Goddess," and *Haramara* for "sea." During their annual pilgrimages to the Pacific Ocean, they deliver sacred objects *(objetos sagradas)*, often arrows embedded with prayers that they then cast into the sea or bury nearby. Upon returning to their villages, they carry seawater with them in bottles for sprinkling on their fields and for use in ceremony.

For ten years, Lena and I studied intensively with a Huichol *maracame* (shaman) named Guadalupe Candelario, until his death in 1999. Over the course of that time, we participated in numerous ceremonies and learned a great deal about the importance of water in the Huichol culture. Guadalupe explained to us that the Huichols, being mostly dry farmers, rely on the sea for the clouds and weather systems that bring rain to water their crops of maize

Yarn painting with snakes

and squash in the arid mountain ranges they call home. According to him, Huichols believe that salamanders are helping spirits who act as midwives to the four Rain Mother Goddesses, especially the one of the east, *Tatei Nariwami*. The salamanders' job is to assist nature by directing the clouds to release their rain in specific places over the land. In their exquisite yarn paintings and beadwork, the Huichols typically depict the rain goddesses as a powerful coiled serpent or as heavy storm clouds out of which millions of tiny snakes descend, symbolizing the life-giving rain.

The Huichols often depict serpents as middlemen between humans and the spirit world and use them to represent a deep intuitive knowledge of nature, especially water. Turtles are emissaries of Tatei Nariwami as well. Their job is to cause the waters to flow, purifying and replenishing ponds, springs, and small bodies of water.

Springs containing *Kuutsala,* beneficial healing waters, are especially sacred to the Huichols, and are important pilgrimage

Huichol yarn painting depicting water or rain

stops for extensive ceremonies. From these springs they obtain the waters they later use in ceremony to purify, cleanse, and revitalize. One of their most sacred springs, *Tatei Matinieri* ("Where our mother is") lies en route to the sacred peyote fields of central Mexico, a destination all Huichols strive to reach during their lifetime.

Guadalupe, like all indigenous peoples, considered water to be the sacred source of life. Without it, he said, nothing on this Earth would be able to survive. He often sang to the spirit of water to thank it for its many gifts; invoke its life-giving waters; and invite its ability to transform, cleanse, and heal.

During ceremonies, I often witnessed Guadalupe placing a small jar of seawater on the altar to bring the spirit of the sea into the ceremony and make her available to all participants. According to him, during the course of an all-night ceremony, the open bowl of water absorbs the songs and prayers chanted by the *maracames,* the shamans presiding over the ceremony. In the morning, Guadalupe would dip a deer-tail wand into the seawater and drip it onto the crowns of our heads and our foreheads, cheeks, wrists, and throats. This, he told me, was meant to both purify us and to embed the prayers and songs of the ceremony into us. In the breezy, freezing dawn light after a sleepless night of smoke, wind, and chanting, the water drops would feel amazingly refreshing. They were like ice trickling down the face and hands as the sun began to bathe the desert in its golden glow.

As with the Shipibo, the Huichols use water as a medium to transport prayers and healing songs into the body of the patient. I've seen Guadalupe pass eagle and hawk feathers over a *hayurame,* an open bottle of water, then sing into it and instruct the patient to drink it as a *remedio* (remedy) throughout the day or over a period of days. He told us that water is friendly to people and supports the transfer of prayers (intentions) and healing energies from other allies, such as the eagle, sun, moon, or stars. Interestingly, other Huichols can tell the difference between plain, unconsecrated water and water into which prayers have been introduced. They can actually see little lights and energy particles dancing in the treated water, whereas the average person can see no difference whatsoever. Most amazing, the Huichols can pick out the prayer water every time.

For Huichols, water isn't a separate or a dead thing, nor is anything in nature isolated. All *poderios* work together, overlapping their energy fields to produce a balanced world where humans, plants, animals, and elements can be in harmony. For example, the Huichols believe that human beings were created by Spirit to be like flowers with blossoms (the crown of the head) open to the sun, supported by a strong vertical stalk (the spinal column). This beautiful flower is, of course, kept alive by an ample supply of water, as all plants are. For this reason, Huichols dress like colorful flowers, the men wearing wide-brimmed hats like gorgeous blossoms in full bloom. They're fond of pouring water onto the crown of the head in ceremony—not to get rid of original sin, as Christians do in baptism, but to introduce life-giving energy to that sacred opening in the head.

TUVAN SHAMANIC UNDERSTANDINGS OF WATER

Now we shift our focus all the way around the world to Mongolia in the northern Asian steppes, where many groups—including Tuvans, Buryat, Hamnigan, Darkhad, Tsaatan, Hotgoit, Urianhai, and the Halh—practice the ancient tradition of shamanism. In particular, our focus will be on the Tuvans, a society of approximately 235,000 people, perhaps most famous for their traditional art of throat singing. Although as of this time I haven't had the opportunity to visit Mongolia personally, I've been able to learn from those who have training in the Tuvan form of shamanism. Their beliefs are remarkably similar to the traditions I have more direct experience with and have already described.

Tuvan shamanism has its origins in the Stone and Bronze Ages, when survival was difficult and specialized tools and practices were needed to cope with a dangerous and hazardous environment. The fact that the Tuvans' shamanic practice has survived to this day is testament to its practicality, effectiveness, and resilience even in the face of attempted eradication at the hands of the

Communists and organized religions. (The Buddhist religion, however, didn't attempt to eliminate it, but rather accommodated it in its practices and beliefs. Buddhism continues to be practiced alongside shamanism to this day.)

Early shamans from this region crossed the Bering Strait during the ice ages and began their migrations into North, Central, and South America. Thus, it's understandable that shamanic insights about the power of water are so similar in such diverse regions of the world.

Tuvans believe that every lake or river has its own spirit keeper or guardian who protects that place and is in charge of the animals and plants living there. They believe that if drawn into alliance through proper respect, these guardian spirits have the ability to protect people living nearby or those who happen to be traveling through the area. The Tuvans believe that guardian spirits of the waters are able to understand the languages of humans and that by speaking or singing directly to them, one can obtain their protection and goodwill.

Like most shamanic peoples, they understand that guardian spirits must be complimented and honored if they're to become good human allies. They erect a small hut *(ovaa)* made of stones and branches on the riverbank near fords in order to house their offerings to the guardian spirits there. (This is similar to the Huichols' temples that contain sacred objects at pilgrimage sites.) Inside, they place sacred stones, crafts, textiles, and blessed objects as forms of sacrifice. This is often carried out prior to attempting to cross the river in order to ensure the safe passage of all the travelers.

The subjects of the Tuvans' songs are usually the elements of nature: the wind in the grasses, ripples on a body of water, rain-laden clouds, and so on. On one occasion, I witnessed traveling throat singers, singing to reproduce the spirit of rain clouds on the distant horizon. They told me that the idea was to make a connection with that element and communicate with it via deep-throated sounds. Thus, like the Shipibo and the Huichols, the Tuvans connect with the spirits of water through their singing practice. By bonding deeply and forming resonance with the water, they honor it and receive its gifts.

The Tuvans hold springs to be especially sacred and consider the trees and plants that grow there to be guarded by the spirit keeper of the spring. Particularly unusual trees growing in these places— ones with double trunks, gnarled survivors of harsh weather, and those clearly struck by lightning—are called "shaman trees" and are given special honor. Under them, the Tuvans perform their ceremonies honoring the springs and asking for their protection and healing gifts. Around such springs, especially medicinal ones, hunting is forbidden in order to keep from offending the guardian of that place, whose protection is extended to the animals there.

Like shamans in many parts of the world, Mongolian shamans practice the shamanic journey, inducing trance states with the use of skin drums. They train for these experiences by stimulating the imagination until it becomes a powerful and useful tool to travel with. Often the trance journey begins at the sacred spring, the entrance point for the three worlds of the spirit realm. As the drumming begins, the shaman imagines himself entering the water of the spring, meeting with the guardian spirit there and communicating his intention or destination. The guardian of the waters then accompanies the shaman on an extensive and sometimes perilous path through underground waterways to a distant landscape where knowledge may be found or power garnered in order to perform healing or a task.

Through the use of this technique, the shaman may meet other powerful spirits, do battle with them, retrieve lost souls, or see into the future. The return journey is typically back through the waterways and out of the spring again. Other shamans may use cave entrances or shaman trees as points of entry into the spirit realm, but entering water is a particularly effective method.

Guided by a woman trained in Tuvan shamanism, I was able to journey via a spring and the underground waterways to discover the answer to an important question about my health. The guardian of the waters I encountered was a beautiful, tall woman who directed me to the shore of a river, where I was led to a small cave and given guidance about my condition. After offering thanks, I returned to the shore, plunged into the river, and went back through the rapidly flowing channels of underground water to the spring where I began the journey. As a result, my health was restored.

Tuvan shamans align themselves with, and draw their power from, particular spirits and become specialists in those elements. Some are more connected with mountains while others are focused on the spirit of water, either in the form of small springs or large bodies such as broad rivers and big lakes. Interestingly, given my own experience, the spirit of water among the Tuvans is typically feminine, and therefore appears to the shamans who work with her as a tall woman with long arms. Sometimes the spirit also appears in the form of a large snake, similar to Roni, the anaconda spirit of the Shipibo.

One of the jobs of the Tuvan shaman is to see that bodies of water are protected from pollution by people. Casting waste or garbage into water is seen as disrespectful and may arouse the ire of the water guardian of that place. For the Tuvans, as with the Shipibo, the spirits of water can be helpful and protective or may be dangerous if not handled properly. Healing often has to do with maladies and illnesses that have come from being careless around sacred bodies of water. On the other hand, the guardian spirit of water can be called upon to free someone of illness, depression, or bad luck. Tuvan shamans understand that these cures may not last forever, so repeat ceremonies may be needed every year or two to continue benefiting from the help of the spirit. In this way, the water spirits are continually honored, and the tradition is perpetuated. Likewise, the shamans understand that their work with spirit through ceremony is a necessary and ongoing practice in order to keep the world in balance.

In this short article, I've touched on the deepest understandings of three different cultures regarding the properties of water. Although remote from one another geographically, all three cultures have remarkably similar beliefs about the nature of water. The Shipibo, the Huichols, and the Tuvans all:

- See water as the giver of life

- Hold water to be sacred

- View water as alive and guided by spirits

- Understand water to be a vehicle or medium of transport for other energies

- Sing to water to make a deep connection and resonance with her

- Use water to heal, purify, and cleanse in ceremony

- Form an alliance with water for assistance and power

- Make offerings of sacred objects to honor water

- Recognize that disrespect toward water can cause negative consequences

- Acknowledge that water has a deep structure that reflects the patterns in nature

If we were to expand our study to include thousands of other shamanically based tribes in the world, we would discover similar if not identical beliefs.

○ ○ ○

BIBLIOGRAPHY

Nevill Drury, *Shamanism,* Longmead: Element Books, 1989.

Mongus Kenin-Lopsan, *Magic of Tuvian Shamans,* Kyzyl: Novosty Tuva, 1993.

Ralph Metzner, *Ayahuasca,* New York: Thunder's Mouth Press, 1999.

Jeremy Narby, *Shamans Through Time,* New York: Tarcher Putnam, 2001.

Sarangerel, *Riding Windhorses: A Journey into the Heart of Mongolian Shamanism,* Rochester, Vermont: Destiny Books, 2000.

Stacey B. Schaefer and Peter T. Furst (eds), *People of the Peyote,* University of New Mexico Press, 1996.

S. I. Serov, "Guardians and Spirit Masters of Siberia" in W. Fitzhugh and A, Crowell (eds), *Cross- roads of Continents,* Washington, DC: Smithsonian Institution Press, 1988.

José and Lena Stevens, *Secrets of Shamanism,* New York: Avon Books, 1988.

WEBSITES

www.thepowerpath.com

www.folklore.ee/folklore/vol4/hoppal.htm

www.buryatmongol.com/msa.html

www.mexconnect.com/mex_/huichol/links.html

○○○ ○○○

"Circe Invidiosa" by John William Waterhouse

CHAPTER 15

WATER LORE AND RITUAL IN WORLD MYTHOLOGY

by Terri Windling

*"Water comes up from the ground, water comes down from the sky.
Water comes into our bodies, water comes out of our bodies. All life
is communicated through water. Nature talks to itself through the
medium of water. We are born in water. We are of water."*[1]
— TOM BLUE WOLF

From my Devon village in the west of England, it's a
short distance through winding green lanes to the once-
independent kingdom of Cornwall—a land of mysterious
standing stones, crumbling Celtic ruins, and ancient stories. On
a bright, clear day near the summer solstice, a friend and I made
a sacred pilgrimage to the Cornish countryside. We went seeking
an ancient magic that lies beneath the surface of the rolling hills:
water magic, pooled in half-forgotten holy wells and springs . . .
found in myths and legends not only in the British Isles, but all
around the world.

A mile or so past the village of Callington, we parked at the
edge of a farmyard and followed an overgrown footpath to Dupath
Well. Like many of the holy wells of Cornwall, the spring that
runs through Dupath Well is believed to have been a sacred site to
Celtic peoples in the distant past, its older use now overlaid with a
gloss of Christian legend. At one time, this spring may have been

surrounded by a grove of oak, rowan, and thorn—trees sacred to the druids and practitioners of other animist religions.

In 1510, a group of Christian monks claimed the Dupath site for their own use, enclosing the spring in a small well house made out of rough-hewn granite. This was the common fate of many pagan sacred sites in the British Isles. Unable to dissuade the local people from visiting their holy places, Christian missionaries simply took them over building churches where standing stones once stood; erecting baptisteries over sacred springs; and cutting down groves of oak, rowan, and thorn in a new god's name. One can still find numerous holy wells buried all over the British countryside, many of them now named for saints and associated with their miraculous lives. But scratch the surface of these legends and older stories emerge like a palimpsest—stories of fairy creatures, the knights of Arthur, and the old gods of the land.

Inside the tiny chapel-like building erected over Dupath Well, the holy water pools in a shallow trough carved from a single granite slab. The air feels thick, heavy with shadows, with silence, with the ghosts of men and women drawn to this spot over hundreds of years. The stones are worn where these people once knelt and prayed to the Virgin Mary, or to the Goddess of the Sacred Springs. At the bottom of the trough lie a few copper

coins—the modern custom of making wishes being not so very different from the pagan practice of throwing pins into a well to ask for blessings. I watch as my companion places an offering of wildflowers by the water—an equally ancient practice recalling a time when it was the land itself our ancestors worshiped, prayed to, and thanked for the gift of life.

ANCIENT WATER MYTHS AND RITUALS

Today, with clean water piped directly into our homes and largely taken for granted, it takes a leap of imagination to consider the greater importance of water to those who fetched it daily from the riverside or village well. Deeply dependent on the local water source for their crops and animals, our ancestors had a natural reverence for those places where good, pure water emerged like magic from the depths of the earth. As a result, water has played a role in myth, folklore, and sacred rites in cultures all around the globe, particularly in arid lands where the gift of water is most precious.

CREATION MYTHS

According to a Blackfoot creation myth, in the beginning there was a great womb containing all of the animals, including Old Man. One day the womb burst, and all creation was underwater. Old Man and the animals emerged floating on a large raft. Old Man suggested that Beaver dive down and try to bring up some mud. Beaver was gone a very long time, but still he couldn't reach the bottom of the water. Loon tried, Otter tried, but the water was just too deep for them. Finally little Muskrat tried. He was gone so long that he was nearly dead when they pulled him onto the raft again, yet he clutched a precious bit of mud in one of his little claws. From this mud, Old Man formed the land that emerged from that great ocean of water, and then he created all of the peoples, trees, and plant life upon it.

"Hylas and Water Nymphs" by John William Waterhouse

We find variations of this "diver motif" myth not only throughout North America but also in cultures around the world, including Buriat cosmology, Finnish folktales, and the Hindu *Paranas*.

WATER GODDESSES AND NATURE SPIRITS

Many cultures associate water with women—with the Great Goddess, or several goddesses, or a variety of female nature spirits. The !Kung of Botswana, for example, attribute the mythic origin of water to women and therefore grant all women special power over water in all its forms. All-mother, in an Aboriginal myth from northern Australia, arrived from the sea in the form of a rainbow serpent with children (the Ancestors) inside her. She made water for the Ancestors by urinating on the land, creating lakes, rivers, and water holes to quench their thirst.

The "living water" (running water) of springs and natural fountains is particularly associated in ancient mythological systems with women, fertility, and childbirth. Greek wells and fountains were sacred to various goddesses and had miraculous powers, such as the fountain at Kanathos, in which Hera regained her virginity each year.

Greek springs were said to be the haunts of water nymphs, elemental spirits shaped like lovely young girls. (The original meaning of the Greek word for *spring* was "nubile maiden.")

In Teutonic myth, the wild wood-wife (a kind of forest fairy) who loves the hero Wolfdietrich is transformed into a human girl when she's baptized in a sacred fountain.

The Norse god Odin seeks wisdom and cunning from the fountain of the nature spirit Mimir. He sacrifices one of his eyes in exchange for a few precious sips of the water.

In Celtic legend, the salmon of knowledge swims in a sacred spring or pool under the shade of a hazel tree; the falling hazelnuts contain all the wisdom of the world and are swallowed by the fish.

RITUAL WASHING

Ritual washing in water or immersion in a pool has been part of various religious systems since the dawn of time. The priests of ancient Egypt washed themselves in water twice each day and twice each night. In Siberia, ritual washing of the body—accompanied by certain chants and prayers—was a part of shamanic practice. In Hinduism, *ghats* are traditional sites for public ritual bathing, an act by which one achieves both physical and spiritual purification [see Chapter 19]. In a strict Jewish household, hands must be washed before saying prayers and before any meal, including bread. In Islam, mosques provide water for the faithful to wash before each of the five daily prayers. In the Christian tradition, baptism is described by Saint Paul as "a ritual death and rebirth which simulates the death and resurrection of Christ." [See Chapter 11.]

FLOOD MYTHOLOGY

In numerous stories, Earth itself is reborn after catastrophic floods. In Greek legend, Zeus sends a flood in which all perish except Deucalion and his wife, who manage to survive by floating in a chest for nine days and nights. Landing on Mount Parnassus, they wisely make a prompt sacrifice to Zeus. The god instructs the obedient couple to throw handfuls of stones over their heads. These turn into a new, better race of men and women, who repopulate the planet.

In Welsh myth, the lake of Llion overflows and drowns the British Isles. One couple escapes in a mastless boat filled with animals like Noah's Ark and lands on dry land at last in Prydain, or modern Wales.

In Persian tales, the world is filled with wicked creatures ruled by the demon Ahriman. An angel, Tistar, comes to Earth three times as a man, a horse, and a bull. Each time he brings ten days and nights of heavy rain, flooding the globe. After several pitched battles with Ahriman, Tistar prevails and the demons are driven from the world; but their poison, flushed from the land, causes the oceans to turn to salt.

In Norse myth, the blood of the ice giant Ymir, who's slain by Odin, causes a massive flood, wiping out most of the ice-giant race. Ymir's body becomes the earth, and his salty blood forms the oceans upon it, creating the world that humankind has inhabited ever since.

India, Africa, Russia, and Tibet—all have ancient tales of monumental floods, after which the blessed (or just plain lucky) members of the human race start anew.

REGENERATION THROUGH WATER

The idea of regeneration through water is echoed in tales around the world about fountains and springs with miraculous powers. The native peoples of Puerto Rico, Cuba, and Hispaniola all told tales of a magical Fountain of Youth located somewhere in the lands to the north. So pervasive were these stories that in the 16th century, the Spanish conquistador Ponce de León actually set out to find it once and for all, equipping three ships at his own expense. He found Florida instead.

One Native American story recounts how the Fountain of Youth is created by two hawks in the netherworld between Heaven

"A mermaid" by John William Waterhouse

and Earth. But this fountain brings grief, as those who drink of it outlive their children and friends, and eventually it's destroyed.

In Japanese legends, the white and yellow leaves of the wild chrysanthemum confer blessings from Kiku-Jido, the chrysanthemum boy who dwells by the Fountain of Youth. These leaves are ceremonially dipped in *sake* to assure good health and long life.

In the Alexander romances, Alexander sets off to find the fabled Fountain of Life in the Land of Darkness beyond the setting sun. The prophet Khizr is his guide, but the two take separate forks in the road and it's Khizr, not his master, who finds the fountain, drinks the water, and obtains knowledge of god. Khizr is still venerated in modern India in both Hindu and Muslim traditions. In Muslim practice, he's honored by lighting lamps and setting them on little boats afloat on rivers and ponds.

To the Celtic people of the British Isles, certain waters were deemed to have healing properties and thus were under divine protection. The famous hot spring at Bath (Aquae Sulis) was dedicated to the goddess Sulis, who was linked from Roman times with one of the Romans' own goddesses to become Sulis Minerva. The Romans built a temple on the site, and a magnificent public bathhouse that still stands today [see Chapter 18].

Chalice Well in Glastonbury is reputed to be among the oldest of the continually used holy wells in Europe; archaeological evidence suggests it has been a sacred site for at least 2,000 years [see Chapter 17].

WATER RITES

The standing stones and circles of Britain are generally found near wells or running water, attesting to the importance of water in pagan religious rites. With the spread of Christianity, a concerted effort was made to stamp out the older animist religions, which attributed divinity to nature. In the 5th century, a canon issued by the Second Council of Arles stated uncategorically that if, in the territory of a bishop, "infidels" lit torches or venerated trees, fountains, or stones, and the bishop neglected to abolish this usage, he was guilty of sacrilege.

Despite the destruction of ancient holy sites, pagan beliefs proved harder to eradicate. By the 7th century, Pope Gregory decided on a new approach and instructed Saint Augustine to convert sacred sites to Christian use. Pagan wells became holy wells, and churches were built upon them or beside them—yet the old ways must have persisted, for in the 10th, 11th, and 12th centuries, a stream of edicts was issued denouncing the worship of "the sun or the moon, fire or flood, wells or stones or any kind of forest tree."

Over time, however, pagan and Christian practices slowly blended together. Wells named after Christian saints were celebrated with festivals and rites on old pagan holy days in ways that wouldn't have been unfamiliar to "heathen" people. On the Isle of Man, for instance, holy wells are still frequented on

August 1, a festival called *Lugnasad* (a day once sacred to the Celtic god Lugh). August 1 is *Lammas* in the Christian calendar, but the older name for the holiday was still in use on the Isle of Man until the 19th century. In Scotland, the well at Loch Maree is dedicated to Saint Malrubha; but its annual rites, involving the sacrifice of a bull, an offering of milk poured on the ground, and coins driven into the bark of a tree, are clearly more pagan in nature.

SACRED WELLS

The custom of "well dressing" is another Christian rite with pagan origins. During these ceremonies (still practiced in Derbyshire and other parts of England), village wells are decorated with pictures made of flowers, leaves, seeds, feathers, and other natural objects. In centuries past, the wells were "dressed" to thank the patron spirit of the well and request good water for the year to come; now the ceremonies generally take place on Ascension Day, and the pictures created to dress the wells are biblical in nature.

As Christian tales were attached to the springs and wells, they became as colorful as any to be found in pagan folklore. Wells were said to have sprung up where saints were beheaded or had fought off dragons, or where the Virgin Mary appeared and left small footprints pressed into the stone. Wells dedicated to Saint Anne were called "granny wells" (because, as the mother of the Virgin Mary, she was the grandmother of Christ), and particular powers concerning fertility and childbirth were attributed to them.

Up until the 19th century, the holy wells of Britain and Europe were still considered to have miraculous properties and were frequently visited by those seeking cures for disease, physical deformity, or mental illness. Other wells were famous for offering prophetic information—generally determined through the movements of the water, leaves floating upon the surface, or fish (or eels) swimming in the depths. At some wells, the water was drunk from circular cups carved out of animal bone, an echo of the cups carved out of human skulls by the ancient Celts. Pins (usually bent), coins, or bits of metal were common offerings. Rags tied to trees around the holy well were another tradition dating back to pagan times. The cloth was symbolic of ill health or misfortune left behind as one departed.

Some wells, known as "cursing wells," were rather less beneficent. Curses were made by dropping special cursing stones into the well, or the victim's name written on a piece of paper or a wax effigy. At the famous cursing well of Ffynnon Elian, in Wales, one could arrange for a curse by paying the well's guardian a fee to perform an elaborate cursing ritual. A curse could also be removed at this same place for a somewhat larger fee.

In the mid-19th century, Thomas Quiller Couch became interested in the history of sacred wells in Britain; he spent much of his life wandering the wilds of his native Cornwall, seeking them out. Extensive notes on this project were discovered among his papers after his death; and in 1884 *The Ancient and Holy Wells of Cornwall* was published by his daughters, the Misses M. and L. Quiller Couch.

More recently, folklorist and photographer Paul Broadhurst revisited the sites documented by Quiller Couch; and in 1988 he published *Secret Shrines: In Search of the Old Holy Wells of Cornwall,* an informative guide to the many sacred wells still to be found in the Cornish countryside.[2] In addition to holy sites dedicated to Celtic goddesses and Christian saints, Broadhurst discovered crumbling old wells half-buried in ivy, bracken, and briars inhabited by spirits somewhat less exalted: the piskies (fairies) of Cornish folklore. Wells under the protection of the piskies are not to be trifled with, for they'll take their revenge on any who dare to disturb their homes. A farmer once decided to move the stone basin at Saint Nun's Well (also known as Piskey's Well), with the intention of using it as a water trough for his pigs. He chained it to two oxen and pulled it the top of a steep hill, whereupon it broke free of the chains, rolled downhill, made a sharp turn right, and settled back into its place. One of the oxen died on the spot, and the farmer was struck lame. This rather enchanted-looking well can still be found in the beautiful part of Cornwall between Liskeard and Looe.

WATER FAIRIES

All running water, not just spring water, can prove to be the haunt of fairies, for crossing over (or through) running water is one of the ways to enter their realm. Here in Devon and Cornwall, one still finds country folk who avoid running water by dusk or dark, for the spirits who inhabit water can be troublesome, even deadly. The water spirit of the River Dart, for instance, is believed to demand sacrificial drownings, leading to the well-known local rhyme: "Dart, Dart, cruel Dart, every year she claims a heart."

The water wraith of Scotland—thin, ragged, and invariably dressed in green—haunts riversides by night to lead travelers to a watery death. In the border country between Scotland and England, the Washer by the Ford wails as she washes the grave clothes of those who are about to die. This frightening apparition is similar to the dreaded *Bean-Sidhe* (Banshee) of Irish legends. The *Bean-nighe* is a similar creature found in both Highland and Irish lore, a dangerous little fairy with ragged green clothes and webbed red feet. (Yet if one can get between the Bean-nighe and her water source, she's obliged to grant three wishes and refrain from doing harm.)

Jenny Greenteeth specializes in dragging children down in stagnant pools. The Welsh water leaper *(Llamhigyn Y Dwr)* is a toadlike creature who delights in tangling fishing lines and devouring any sheep who fall into the river. The *fideal* is a fairy who haunts lonely pools and hides herself in the grasses by the water; the *glaistig,* half woman and half goat, tends to lurk in the dark of caves behind waterfalls. The *loireag* of the Hebrides is a gentler breed of water fairy, although as a connoisseur of music even she can prove dangerous to those who dare to sing out of tune.

In Ireland, a fairy woman known as the Lady of the Lake bestows blessings and good weather to those who seek her favor; in some towns she's still celebrated (or propitiated) at midsummer festivals. Her name recalls the Welsh Lady of the Lake who gave King Arthur his sword and now guards his body as he sleeps in Avalon.

Brittany, on the west coast of France, also claims to be the home of the Lady of the Lake. The Château de Comper, where she's said to have lived and raised Sir Lancelot, still stands near the old Forest of Paimpont (called *Broceliande* in Arthurian lore), a magnificent manor house of golden stone, crumbling romantically at the edges. Nearby is a lake whose origin is attributed to Morgan Le Fay, located in the mysterious Val sans Retour (Valley of No Return).

Chalice Well in Glastonbury is one of several sites where the Holy Grail is reputed to be hidden. At the foot of ancient Glastonbury Tor is a lovely garden where one can drink the red-tinged water of the well—colored, according to legend, by the blood of Christ carried in the Grail [see Chapters 8 and 17].

Although the well's association with Arthur may be, as some Arthurian scholars suggest, a legend of recent vintage, archaeological excavations in the 1960s established the site's antiquity—and the place manages to retain a tranquil, mystical atmosphere despite its transformation from sacred site to tourist attraction. One often finds small offerings in the circle around the well's heavy lid: flowers, feathers, stones, small bits of cloth tied to a nearby tree . . . remnants of ancient pagan practice carried down through the centuries.

THE ROLE OF WATER TODAY

In modern times, we generally view such practices as quaintly (or foolishly) superstitious; we dismiss our early ancestors as ignorant savages who worshipped natural phenomena because they lacked the rationality of science. Yet a look at the animist religions that still thrive in many cultures around the globe indicates that this may be a simplistic view of nature-based religions [see Chapter 14]. Rather than focusing on the hocus-pocus of the supernatural (as they're often portrayed), such religions are rooted in the natural world, celebrating and regulating the relationships between humankind, other species, and the land that sustains us all.

In America, animism runs through the indigenous religions of the land. Various springs, wells, and pools are sacred to Native American tribal groups; and in such holy places one finds offerings similar to those by Chalice Well: feathers, flowers, stones, sage, tobacco, small carved animal forms, scraps of red cloth tied to trees, and other tokens of prayer. The Native American sweat-lodge ceremony uses water sprinkled over red-hot rocks to create the steam that's called the "breath of life." The lodge itself is the womb of Mother Earth, in which one is washed clean, purified, and spiritually reborn. In Native American church ceremonies, a pail of "Morning Water" is traditionally carried and prayed over by a woman before being sent sunwise around the circle to be shared by all. Water is sacred through its absence in the four-day Sundance ceremony, or the ritual of Crying for a Vision. After four days without water (or food), the first drop on the tongue is a potent reminder to be thankful for this precious gift from Mother Earth.

Tom Blue Wolf of the Eastern Lower Muscogee Creek Nation speaks of the central importance of water, particularly at a time when water tables worldwide are diminishing at alarming rates:

> Once upon a time, the Chattahoochee River was known to the people here as the source of life. Every morning we would go to the water and fill ourselves with gratitude, and thank the Creator for giving us this source of life. We would honor it throughout the day. At that time, water was known as the Long Man. It came from a place that has no beginning, and went to a place that had no end. But now, for the first time in the history of our people, we can see the end of water.[3]

Mythologist Michael Meade takes note of the ancient symbolism of water, and its vital role in our lives today:

> Of the elements—which some people count as four, and others count as five—water is the element for reconciliation. Water is the element of flow. When water goes missing, flow goes missing. The ancient Irish used to say that there were two suns in the world. One you see rise in the morning. The other is very deep in the Earth, and it's called the black sun or inner sun. It's a hot fire in there; no one knows how hot. The Earth is roughly 70 percent water because of that hidden sun inside. When the water goes down, the Earth heats up too much—part of the global warming that's happening everywhere. It happens inside people also, because people are like the Earth. People are 70 percent water,

like the Earth, and people have a hidden sun—or else we wouldn't be 96° when it's 40° outside. Everyone in the world is burning, and the water in the body keeps that burning from becoming a fever. What happens literally also happens emotionally and spiritually, so when people forget how to carry water and how to use water to reconcile, you get an increasing amount of heated conflict, as we're seeing around the world today. . . . In many cultures it's the elders who carry the water, because elders are the peace-bringers. When a culture can't remember or imagine peace on its streets or how to negotiate peace, it means its elders have forgotten what to do, how to carry water.[4]

The following evocative words come from a film about Chief Seattle, depicting the forced transfer of Suquamish lands to the U.S. government in 1855:

> The shining water that moves in the streams and rivers is not just water, but the blood of our ancestors. If we sell you our land, you must remember that it is sacred. Each ghostly reflection in the clear water of the lakes tells of events and memories in the life of my people. The water's murmur is the voice of my father's father. The rivers are our brothers. They quench our thirst. They carry our canoes and feed our children. So you must give to the rivers the kindness you would give any brother . . . This we know: the Earth does not belong to man, man belongs to the Earth.[5]

I'm reminded here, at Dupath Well, that I, too, have distant ancestors who didn't consider themselves greater than the land on which they lived; didn't take good, pure water for granted; and who knew humans belonged to the earth.

An old English folklorist told me once that nature spirits would live in a well, a spring, a lake, or a grove of trees only as long as they were remembered and addressed respectfully. If the spirits were neglected, they'd leave the place; the land would feel soulless and dead henceforth. Remembering this, I dropped a pin into the brown water of Dupath Well. The well house stands near a farmyard. I could hear the traffic of the roads nearby, and yet somehow the spot still seemed timeless, magical—and very much alive. I cupped my hands, drank from the well, and whispered, "Thank you," as I left. I couldn't even tell you now who exactly I was addressing—a nature spirit, a well fairy, a Celtic goddess, or the earth itself. And yet, in that ancient place, I swear that someone was listening.

○ ○ ○

NOTES

1. Tom Blue Wolf and Michael Meade, "The Big Story: The Return of Sophia" lecture, the second Mythic Journeys conference, Atlanta, Georgia, June 2006; **www.mythicjourneys.org**.

2. Paul Broadhurst, *Secret Shrines: In Search of the Old Holy Wells of Cornwall*, Mythos Publishers, 1988.

3. Tom Blue Wolf, *op. cit.*

4. Michael Meade, *ibid.*

5. The speech has been erroneously attributed to Chief Seattle himself. More information on the subject can be found at **www.kyphilom.com/www/seattle.html**.

FURTHER READING

David Abrams, *Spell of the Sensuous,* Vintage, 1997.

Janet and Colin Bord, *Sacred Waters: Holy Wells and Water Lore in Britain and Ireland,* Granada, 1985.

Mary G. Brenneman and Walter L. Vrenneman, Jr., *Crossing the Circle at the Holy Wells of Ireland,* University of Virginia Press, 1995.

Paul Broadhurst, *Secret Shrines: In Search of the Old Holy Wells of Cornwall,* Mythos Publishers, 1988.

Michael P. Carroll, *Irish Pilgrimage: Holy Wells and Popular Catholic Devotion,* John Hopkins University Press, 2000.

Arthur Gribben, *Holy Wells and Sacred Water Sources in Britain and Ireland,* Garland, 1992.

Flora Gregg Iliff, *People of the Blue Water,* University of Arizona Press, reprint edition, 1985.

Francis Jones, *The Holy Wells of Wales,* University of Wales Press, 2003.

Michael J. Meade, *Men and the Water of Life,* HarperCollins, 1993.

Gary Nabhan, *The Desert Smells Like Rain,* University of Arizona Press, reprint edition, 2002.

James Rattue, *The Living Stream: Holy Wells in Historical Context,* The Boydell Press, 1995.

Snejana J. Tempest, *Water: Folk Belief, Ritual and the East Slavic Wondertale,* Yale University, 1993.

CHAPTER 16

LOURDES AND OTHER HEALING
WELLS AND SPRINGS ASSOCIATED
WITH GODDESSES AND FEMALE SAINTS

by Doreen Virtue, Ph.D.

O f the four earthly elements, water and earth have long been considered feminine, while air and fire are regarded as masculine elements. Women, as childbearers, are associated with the life-giving flow of rivers, streams, springs, and wells. Cross-culturally, water is a symbol of fertility and prosperity. So it's logical that our ancestors built water-based shrines in honor of divine feminine goddesses and female saints.

Archaeologists have discovered water wells with spiritual and religious themes dating back to the late Bronze Age, which are reputed to have healing properties. The root word for *well* is *wella, wielle,* or *waella,* which in Old English means "natural spring" or "moving water." So a healing well could be a thermal spring, or the head of a river or stream. Rivers named for healing goddesses are abundant throughout Europe, including the Danube, which was named for the Celtic Mother Goddess Danu; and the Seine, named for the Gallo-Roman healing goddess Sequana.

Healing wells and springs are found worldwide, but are particularly abundant in Europe. Ireland reportedly has more than 3,000 healing wells. Many of these are dedicated to Brigit, a healing goddess who was later adopted and canonized by the Catholic church.

The most famous healing spring is undoubtedly Lourdes in southern France, dedicated to Mother Mary. Scientists have verified 66 healings at Lourdes, and an estimated 50 unverified healings per month are reported.

Another famous healing spring is in Bath, England. This 10,000-year-old shrine was originally erected in honor of the Roman goddess Minerva, and later became dedicated to the Celtic water goddess Sulis [see Chapter 18].

Many healing wells were created during pre-Christian eras. They were dedicated to Hindu, Roman, Celtic, Egyptian, Mayan, and other goddesses (and occasional gods) to appease and appeal for favors, healings, divination, and protection. During the Crusades, many European wells were rededicated to saints. Roman and Celtic wells dedicated to the goddess Coventina were converted into "wishing wells." The previous Roman practice of throwing sacrificial animals into the well to win Coventina's favor was replaced with tossing in coins or floating votive candles to elicit good luck.

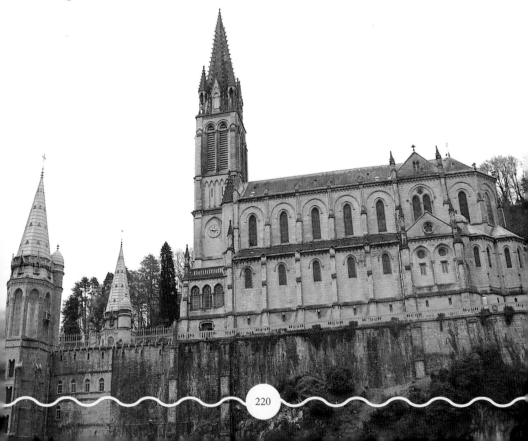

Specific wells and their associated goddesses and saints gained reputations as having healing specialties. Many of these locations were attributed with miraculous abilities to heal eyesight, which some believe had to do with the vitamin and mineral content of spring water. Others were reputed to restore fertility, heal toothaches, skin diseases, and other illnesses and injuries.

I've personally visited several healing wells dedicated to goddesses and saints. Each time, I've noticed intense feelings of positive energy near these waters. Going to the well (known as a "grotto") at Lourdes was a particularly powerful experience for me. Standing near the water felt as intense as being in a room filled with magnets drawing impurities out of my body, mind, and emotions. I witnessed people wheeled on gurneys and saw their beaming smiles as their nurses bathed them in the sacred waters. I brought home some Lourdes water and gave bottles to friends, one of whom reported the immediate healing of an injury after she'd splashed the water on it.

Studies on the properties, effects, and electrical fields of Lourdes and other healing wells have been conducted by scientists. Dr. Enzo Ciccolo, a biologist at the University of Milan, collected water from wells where Mother Mary apparitions had been sighted, including Lourdes, Medjugorje in Croatia, Fatima in Portugal, and Montichiari and San Damiano in Italy.

Dr. Ciccolo placed small quantities of these Marian waters (named for Mother Mary) into normal tap water. The tap water's pH, conductivity, and redox potential were immediately modified by the addition of the Marian water. Researcher A. Ansaloni also found that tap water's pH level reduced with the addition of one part Lourdes water to 400,000 parts tap water. In addition, Ansaloni discovered that Lourdes water slowed the decay of chlorine in water, no matter how small of a sample of Lourdes water was added to the chlorinated water.

Dr. Ciccolo noted that after people bathed in Lourdes water, it became cloudy, as if the bather had detoxified into it. A study of the residue in the water revealed that the pathogens were neutralized:

A photoelectronic spectroscopy revealed that all frequencies of light were present in that sample of water, a phenomenon which usually never occurs in water. In fact, it was precisely this perfect, extraordinary and powerful set of frequencies which prevented the pathogenic germs from reacting and becoming harmful.[1]

Other scientists have measured Lourdes water using a Bovis scale, which detects life-force energy. Using the earth's energy as a baseline, a substance with fewer than 6,500 Bovis energy units is considered to have a negative or life-detracting charge. Between 6,500 and 8,000 units is thought to be neutral; and 8,000 and above is positive or life affirming. Lourdes water has been measured at 500,000 Bovis energy units.

Interestingly, the particles of negative substances spin clockwise, while positively charged particles spin counter-clockwise. Goddess traditions teach that feminine energy spins to the left or counterclockwise.

Dr. Ciccolo also experimented with water from Medjugorje, Croatia, another healing shrine devoted to Mother Mary, adding small quantities of its water to solutions of sodium chloride, albumin, and cupric chloride and comparing these mixtures to control samples. The Medjugorje samples crystallized into more finely divided filamentary patterns than the control solutions. Dr. Ciccolo noted that the crystallized patterns resembled those that had been observed in samples treated by healers' bioenergy and by magnetic fields.

In other words, water from healing wells associated with Mother Mary is structurally different from other water. Marian water stores the heartfelt prayers and the loving energy associated with Mother Mary and the angels. The studies show that this energy is transferable to ordinary water.

The ancient practice of seeking health through water while invoking the loving help of a goddess or saint remains a popular practice. Between five and six million people visit Lourdes annually. Thousands drink from or swim in the River Ganga, which Hindus regard as the embodiment of Ganga Ma, Saravati, Lakshmi, and other healing goddesses [see Chapter 19]. The ancient Hindu *Vedas* prescribe running water as the means of carrying away physical pollution to attain health.

The universality of visiting healing wells associated with goddesses and saints shows that it's more than a religious practice. The magnetic appeal of healing wells seems to be deeply ingrained. Perhaps it's a human instinct to seek our Divine Mother when we need comfort and healing.

○ ○ ○

NOTES

1. Enzo Ciccolo, "Domenica del Corriere," Cooperative Nuova, Milan, Feb. 18, 1988.

BIBLIOGRAPHY

Doreen Virtue, Ph.D., *Goddesses & Angels,* Hay House, 2005.

——, *Angel Medicine,* Hay House, 2005

○ ○ ○ ○ ○ ○

Chapter 17

CHALICE WELL, GLASTONBURY

by William Bloom, Ph.D.

The English landscape is known for its rolling and soft beauty and for its unexpected and spectacular vistas. You may turn a corner or reach a peak and suddenly, unfolding far into the distance, is a long and intriguing view. One of the greatest of these vistas can be found when you travel south from Bristol and Bath in the west of England. As you pass over the top of the Mendip Hills, before you stretches the large plain of the Mid-Somerset Levels. This is a flat landscape some 15 miles across, which at several points in its history has been covered in water—and may be again. At the center of this flatland is an island whose most prominent feature is a dramatic 500-foot hill with a tower upon its summit. This is Glastonbury.

Also known as the Isle of Avalon, it's one of the most sacred landscapes in Europe. It's the burial place of King Arthur and Queen Guinevere, and the Holy Grail is said to be hidden here. It was a major center of Druidic and pre-Christian spirituality. In the shape of the isle can be found the form of a great goddess, while a vast zodiac can be seen in the landscape surrounding it, carved into the contours of the land. It's the site of the earliest of Christian churches founded, so the legend goes, by Jesus' uncle, Joseph of Arimathea. This small church evolved to become the greatest abbey in all Christendom. The Isle of Avalon, also called the Isle of Glass, was also said to be the capital city of the fairie realm, a great claim for a country known as Angel-Land or England.

The island of Glastonbury is made up of several hills. Three of them are well known: Wearyall Hill, Chalice Hill, and the Tor.

Each of these has a very different shape and atmosphere. Wearyall is long and slim, like a fish, and is known as a place that's good for peace and reflection. Chalice Hill is soft and round, shaped like a breast or pregnant womb, and holds an atmosphere of healing. The Tor is masculine and dramatic, accentuated by its tower; and its energy is powerful and dynamic. People often comment on how these three hills and their characters reflect the trinity found in many spiritual traditions.

The small town of Glastonbury itself sprawls on the island overlit by these hills, its inhabitants divided into those who honor the spirituality of the landscape—I'm one of them, and lucky enough to live on the side of Wearyall Hill—and those who live there as if it were any other small country town.

One of Glastonbury's most intriguing features is to be found in the valley between Chalice Hill and the Tor, down which runs a small road. Near the bottom of this road, on the right side toward Chalice Hill, there's a lovingly tended public garden, the main feature of which is the Chalice Well, previously known as Blood Spring. On the other side of the road, in a nondescript building, is the White Spring.

The waters for each of these two springs have unique sources, and their chemical content is completely different. I've lived in Glastonbury for 30 years and am fascinated by the polarity and paradox of these two wells. Their contrast is so great that many people who visit Chalice Well Gardens—for nurture, inspiration, and meditation—may not even know that the White Spring exists at all.

The water of Chalice Well, Blood Spring, is good for the health. It has an iron content similar to that of human blood, and the flow runs strong and consistently even in periods of drought. As the water surfaces out of the earth, the way in which it's contained and then channeled has been lovingly constructed by human intervention over many centuries. The actual source of the water, the well itself, is capped by a large lid, on which is the ancient symbol of two interlinking circles, the *vesica piscis*. The water then runs through a lion's head, down through some shallow baths for healing, through a Steiner-inspired flow form and into a large pool, again in the shape of the vesica piscis. The surrounding gardens are tended by men and women sensitive to the elements of nature, the Green Man, Pan, and the Goddess, as well as to the fairies, nature spirits, and landscape energies.

Chalice Well

The White Spring, however, has a certain chaos surrounding it; and the human involvement often seems harsh, in my opinion. This may, of course, be totally appropriate—a perfect balance.

Many people have a simple relationship with Chalice Well. They just love it and are grateful for its peace. They quench their thirst and enjoy the atmosphere of the flowing water and the garden's nature spirits. My relationship with the well is more complex. The whole landscape of Glastonbury is filled with symbolism and meaning. For many of its citizens, it's like living inside a pack of tarot cards, each aspect of its landscape filled with metaphor and significance. What then is the role of Chalice Well? How intriguing that it flows with blood between the polarities of Chalice Hill and the Tor. Is this the blood of Christ from the hidden grail? From the Goddess?

The water comes from a deep, powerful, consistent source. Sometimes I imagine this to be the heart of a great dragon miles below in the earth. But why does the creature release some of its blood here? What's the connection? It's interesting to sit in the garden and contemplate the origins of the flow, deep in the earth. Water is alive—not just in its molecular and subatomic structure, but also in the forms it takes. Rivers, lakes, seas, oceans, wells, and springs are all beings in their own right. Who is this being who surfaces at Chalice Well? Of course, this type of question is well asked of any body of water, but first the enquirer must pause and form a relationship with the water.

I often wonder what Blood Spring looked like before any human being had begun to organize it. Its geology isn't rocky or hard. I imagine there was mud and bubbling. It would have spread into the surrounding grassland, and then perhaps channeled away in several directions—uncontrolled, free, and natural.

To the human eye, concerned with a civilized aesthetic sensibility, the messiness of mud and an endless oozing and spreading may seem unattractive compared to the form of a well-tended garden. But it's good for people to play with mud and experience the primal sensations of life. There's no tended garden in a mother's womb, but the environment is luscious and perfect. So sometimes a primal part of me feels a haunted loss when I encounter the neatness and containment of the well and its gardens. But I also recognize the practical need for easier access to the water. I understand why Blood Spring transformed into Chalice Well; and in general, I appreciate the beauty of gardens created by humanity in rapport with nature.

There is, however, another issue for me. It has to do with spirits. I wonder, when the Blood Spring waters were first contained and channeled, whether people offered prayers and ceremonies to ask permission of the spirits of the water and of the land. I wonder whether the great creature who's the whole form and being of this powerful source was ever courted. At every successive stage of the well's construction down the centuries, did the builders have the sensitivity and courtesy to continue these ceremonies and communications of permission and gratitude?

When I first encountered Chalice Well many years ago, ceremonies weren't happening; and the first Warden of the Well, whom I knew, wasn't a happy man. The atmosphere of the gardens was strained. Over recent decades, however, the culture of the custodianship has transformed into one that's attuned to and respectful of the nature spirits, the earth energies, and the life of the water itself. Instinctively and lovingly, ceremonies and communications are happening today; and the governing community of the well is generally, I gather, harmonious. There has been a healing here of the relationship between humans and the spirits of this water. To me, the spirits of this water seem happy now. There's still perhaps some healing needed in the bigger picture and in the relationship with White Spring, but I feel confident that this will come, too.

All this is a lesson, one that's echoing through this entire book: We need to reawaken our care for and relationship with nature and the elements. Without us, the elements flow, explode, emerge, cycle, recycle, die, and are reborn. This is the dance of life. With water, it's all so visible and touchable—the movement, the play, and the power. We love water, but meaningful love is always love in action.

○ ○ ○

BIBLIOGRAPHY

William Bloom and Marko Pogacnik, *Ley Lines and Ecology,* **www.williambloom.com**, 2001.

Frances Howard-Gordon, *Glastonbury: Maker of Myths,* Gothic Image, 1995.

Kathy Jones, *In the Nature of Avalon,* Ariadne Publications, 2000.

Katherine Maltwood, *Glastonbury's Temple of the Stars,* James Clarke, 1982.

Nicholas Mann, *Energy Secrets of Glastonbury Tor,* Green Magic, 2004.

John Michell, *New Light on the Ancient Mystery of Glastonbury,* Gothic Image, 1997.

WEBSITES

www.chalicewell.org.uk

www.williambloom.com

✿✿✿ ✿✿✿

CHAPTER 18

THE DREAMING POOL OF BATH

by Richard Beaumont

Looking earthward, the densely wooded valley couldn't have concealed the ancient river snaking through it. Closer inspection of the serpentine bend would have revealed to prehistoric people a truly awesome sight: clouds of steam billowing out from England's only three hot springs. Mingled with the steam would have been the pungent smell of minerals. The ground soft and boggy, the night sky illuminated by stars playing hide-and-seek through the steam, the sounds of woodland creatures screeching and scratching near and far—it would have been like a dream, an entrance to another world, an underworld, a magical place of initiation. . . .

A MAGICAL HISTORY

In almost two decades of researching mind, body, and spirit subjects, I've encountered many interesting and wonderful people, places, and techniques for self-discovery. One of the strangest encounters followed my interview with Margaret Marion Stewart of the Springs' Foundation.

Margaret was a guide to the Bath springs: Cross Bath Spring, the Hetling Spring, and the King's Spring. She gave guided tours of the Cross Bath. R. J. Stewart, author of *Waters of the Gap*,[1] had told her about the origins of the springs. His research had shown them to be a pre-druidic sacred place, oracular mystery school, and underworld initiation center.

According to Celtic legend, in the 9th century B.C., a chieftain called Bladud was expelled from court because his leprosy made him so ill that he was unable to rule. He became a swineherd instead. One day he followed a scabby pig to the springs and watched as it wallowed in the hot mud and emerged with its pink complexion restored. He plunged in himself and was cured. (The pig is the cult animal of Ceridwen, the goddess of the cauldron of inspiration and immortality.) Bladud is believed to have set up the first academy at the Bath springs around 800 B.C.; and the arts, astronomy, mathematics, astrology, prophecy, divination, and necromancy were taught there.

Margaret told of a legendary place referred to by the Greeks that was beyond Hyperborea, beyond the north wind. It was a triangular island that had two crops a year and hot springs gushing at the center. She felt sure that these were the Bath springs. Reinforcing the Greek connection, there are stories that druids from Bath taught Pythagoras.

The area around the springs would have been sacred, with the public possibly only accessing it at festival times connected with the eightfold calendar. The pre-Roman Celtic culture would have been matriarchal and matrilineal; the sun would have been regarded as feminine, the hot springs as waters from the womb of the Goddess. A volunteer for the Springs' Foundation said, "I really believe it's sacred." She also revealed that since being involved with the spring, "I've felt completely protected. When I have difficulties in my life, I go to the spring, and things work out." This Goddess spirituality is undoubtedly of considerable importance to some in Bath.

During an excavation of the springs in the late 1970s, pre-Roman artifacts were discovered—coins and offerings going back 7,000 years. There were also the remains of the walls the Romans had built around the springs. They paid homage to the local deity by calling the site *Aquae Sulis* (Waters of Sulis) in honor of the Celtic goddess Sulis (*sulis* means "an opening," "an orifice," "an eye," or "a gap"). They built a temple there, incorporating the ancient Celtic site, and dedicated it to Sulis Minerva. (Minerva is the nearest equivalent Roman goddess to Sulis, a goddess of wisdom, healing, and war.)

West of the larger King's Spring, linked to it by a sacred grove, lies the Cross Bath. Margaret's sense of its function was that it was an inner sanctuary. An earlier excavation had revealed part of an altar stone dedicated to Aesculapius, the Greco-Roman god of healing, who presided over *aesculapia,* dream healing temples, where people had a ritual bath and then slept nearby. (Evidence of sheltering cubicles has been discovered under what's now a modern shopping center.) They would have discussed their dreams with the resident therapeuts of the Romano-Celtic period—a sort of early form of psychoanalysis.

From medieval times to the 18th century, the Cross Bath was known as *Balneum Crucis* (Bath of the Cross). It was part of a pilgrimage route between the Glastonbury and Malmesbury abbeys. The pilgrims would carry a life-sized replica of the cross and stop at certain points on the journey. One of the stopping places was the nearby Saint John's Hospital, built by the Knights Templar in 1174. At the time, it was a hospitality place, but such spots eventually became known as hospitals because so many travelers were sick. At the Cross Bath, the pilgrims would have a ritual bath in the healing waters before going on refreshed.

It's also reported that many queens visited the Cross Bath over the years, including Queen Mary; and the town itself became known as Royal Bath in the early 17th century when James I's queen, Anne of Denmark, visited, bathed, and soon conceived. An 18th-century author of a guide to the baths suggested that the waters might well act as a miraculous cure for infertility.

Bath became a fashionable resort of Georgian England under Beau Nash, the legendary master of ceremonies; and in 1822 a doctor with a lucrative practice treating wealthy neurotics in the town said the water was a sovereign cure for "rheumatic, gouty, and paralytic afflictions, in all those disorders originating from indigestion and acidity of the stomach, bilious and glandural obstructions, hypochondriac and hysterical afflictions." By that time, many townsfolk were making a living off the waters, providing cures ranging from cups of steaming water to hot water enemas, selling souvenirs, housing invalids, or carrying them in "Bath chairs" through the streets.

In the 1970s, that all stopped. In 1976, the National Health Service stated that plunging patients into the miraculous water was no more effective than turning on a hot tap, and in 1978 tragedy struck. The water at the King's Spring was found to be polluted, and a girl died of a meningitis-related illness. Bathing ended overnight, and visitors to the Roman baths museum were warned against touching the water.

DREAMS OF INTERVENTION

In 1979, Margaret Stewart started a campaign to reopen the Cross Bath for bathing. The effort gained considerable momentum . . . and then the dreams began.

In one dream, Margaret found herself inside the Cross Bath surrounded by many nonhuman "inner plane" beings. Her sense of privilege at being there amidst so many magnificent creatures turned to dismay and embarrassment as the largest of these beings told her that she was to stop her campaigning and that the baths were meant to be closed at that time. She contacted all the protesters and ended the process the next day.

On reflection, she believed that the baths needed to be closed for a period of inner purification. In the time since bathing had been prohibited, there'd been a change in the springs' temperature. The three springs are all from the same aquifer in oolithic limestone (nonsulfurous, nonvolcanic). The Cross Bath Spring is the deepest at 1.8 miles and used to be the coolest, at 103°F; the Hetling Spring was the hottest at 120°F; the King's Spring was 115°F. Today all the springs have a similar temperature around 111°F.

A recent mineralogical analysis of the hot springs has shown that all the thermal water contains sodium, calcium, chloride, and sulfate ions in high concentrations. Although there are some small variations, allowing for changes in analytical methods, the composition has remained constant over the past century.

When a borehole was put into the King's Spring (the source of the largest volume of water) to get amoeba-free water, Margaret formed the Springs' Foundation to stop plans to cap the Cross

Bath Spring and take water from the King's Spring borehole and pump it into the Cross Bath. As each of the springs comes up from different fissures, they each have slightly different mineral constituents; and Margaret wanted to retain the integrity of the Cross Bath water. As a result of her action, another borehole was made into the Cross Bath Spring's source to provide amoeba-free water to the Cross Bath.

The Springs' Foundation has since seen modern-day pilgrims from all over the world find their way to the Cross Bath and feel blessed.

I'd come to Bath to report on a story about Margaret's fears that the springs might be tapped off and replaced by ordinary heated water from the main water supply. As I listened to her talk about the importance of protecting the site, I remember letting my right hand play in the hot water. It felt thick and strangely "pregnant" with life. It made my fingers tingle.

Four hours later, Margaret was still talking—about the strange dreams that had brought her to be a protector of the site, about unusual winds that had thrown the planners' only redesigns into the water, and about the sudden illnesses that had afflicted the key proponents of the unwanted refurbishment. Having failed to bring the "interview" to a polite end, I took the only option available: I abruptly informed her that I was leaving and, with her voice still echoing behind me, walked away. What I'd imagined would be a pleasant hour-long interview had turned into a four-hour experience of extraordinary mania.

By now I was feeling very strange, and the world around me was echoing this, becoming somehow dreamlike and viscously fluid in a most disconcerting way. As I walked to my car, the night seemed darker than it should have been against the lights of the city.

Upon returning home, I felt an uncharacteristic need to go directly to sleep. What I didn't realize at the time was that I, too, had been affected by the water and was about to experience its power—whether I wanted to or not.

THE GREEN MAN

As soon as I lay down, my entire body seemed leaden; and I fell into a deep, deep state. I could smell waterweeds and see many light-bodied nature spirits wafting around me, almost as if they were preparing the ground for something. A sense of timelessness pervaded the room. As the "dream" began to take a dark turn, I found myself unable to move. Earthy, troll-like characters gathered around me in a circle, their solid frames immovable and glistening with a pale bluish-green light. All these beings were strangely, intimately, familiar to me. They seemed almost like cousins or family: I "knew" which tribe they belonged to, and I "knew" each one of them and they were dear to me; yet I hadn't seen them for longer than I could remember.

Then, with slow methodical progress, a being of immense size and power—ancient beyond my comprehension—came toward us. Imagine a grizzly bear 100 times bigger than any bear you've ever seen, but with an almost human articulation to him. He had to bend down to see me; I was so small in comparison to him. His face seemed as far away as the clouds, but his presence permeated everything. I could feel his breath on my face, and he snorted like a horse. He, too, was familiar, but I'd never before had his attention focused on me alone. It was overpowering. He turned his head from side to side as if trying to understand what I was doing there.

When he spoke, everything around us moved; and the wind of his words flew over my head. It was almost deafening, and yet somehow silent at the same time. It pervaded my whole body. I was "told," wordlessly, but in no uncertain terms, that I had a job to do; and there was no backing out of it. I felt his eyes see right through to my essence. He seemed immortal, immensely wise, and as compassionate as one would be to a creature far lower on the evolutionary chain who'd gotten lost. I also can't forget a feeling of deep sadness emanating from him. I've never felt so "merely" human, so puny, so completely out of my depth.

I woke with a start, soaked with sweat. I felt tiny and insignificant beside such an ancient power. The entire room seemed different and unfamiliar to me. There was no comfort, no assurance that I'd simply had a dream. My reality seemed entirely insubstantial in comparison to what I'd just experienced. I knew with absolute certainty that there was nowhere on Earth where he couldn't find me. It was daylight; I'd "slept" for ten hours, but it felt like 15 minutes.

I got out of bed and the sense of urgency was so great that I called Margaret even before getting dressed. At first it was hard to speak—my voice seemed disconnected from my body, as if I were an actor using a foreign accent—but I now felt a connection to her, knowing that we'd both encountered the same beings. And I had compassion for her, as she was connecting with them on a regular basis. It was no wonder that she'd become so fixated on being a guardian of the waters. She'd seen hundreds of people receive healing from the springs, and knew intimately the powers behind that wonder.

I told her that I was going to run the story and was just calling to check a few details. In the long conversation that ensued, she added yet more information about the complexities of water analyses, microbiological filtering systems, and town-council plans for redevelopment of the springs. I knew I had to pull it all together—premonitions, mythology, history, excavations, water analysis, the lot. I didn't dare cross the ancient being I'd just met.

The result of my labor is in print for all to see.[2] I felt driven throughout the writing of the piece and never lost the strange sense of being in the flow of the fates. As soon as I'd finished the article, I walked toward my kitchen through an enclosed passageway, hearing something calling me. There, for the first and last time in the three years I lived on those premises, I met a huge frog. Its loud croaking filled the sealed corridor, and a tingle went down my spine. The force of nature had sent a messenger. The spell had been completed; the job was done.

THE MYSTERY OF WATER

In our current study of water, especially with Dr. Emoto's discovery of the effect of thought and prayer upon water crystals, there are two paradigms at work, and they don't necessarily mix.

On the one hand, there's science, with its reliance on neutral, objective evidence and logical conclusions. But there's also the mystical experience of those in touch with natural forces, which defies logical definitions, as its interpretations are both universally applicable and yet subjectively personal.

We know that water holds memory. It's also the requisite for all life on this planet. Dr. Emoto's work has demonstrated the effect of our consciousness on water, but what if water isn't simply the receptively inert medium his studies demonstrate? If it can indeed become altered by the consciousness directed at it, isn't it also possible that it could contain and project a more evolved consciousness? Certainly I believe that we should include in our studies of water an investigation into the shamanistic practices upheld even today in the more remote areas of the world, where water blessings still hold their power and human understanding isn't regarded as the pinnacle of awareness.

In our scientific attempts to define and understand matter, we may well have become blind to a direct, more potent way of perceiving the world around us. Can we truly claim to have a fully comprehensive understanding of life without incorporating the experiences of the countless mystics who point to a paradigm beyond intellectual understanding?

THE CURRENT DAY

My meeting with Margaret Stewart took place in 1998. Much has happened since that time. The council's plan for the redevelopment

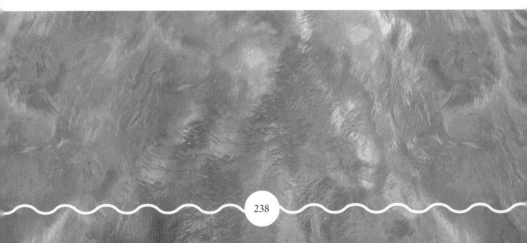

Roman baths in Bath, England

of the springs met with years of bitter wrangling. Petitions were signed for and against it. There was strong local opposition, which led to the threat of legal action against the local authority and the developers, but the case was settled out of court. An uneasy truce was established, giving residents priority access and reduced prices to the restored Georgian Cross Bath. Construction work on the project began and Thermae Bath Spa finally opened in August 2006.[3] Margaret eventually came around to the idea of the refurbishment of the Cross Bath on the basis that "the Goddess is getting a facelift."

The development, which eventually cost $43 million (£23 million), around 50 percent more than its original budget, is certainly impressive. The new spa, the only one in Britain where visitors are able to bathe in naturally heated mineral water, is a combination of new-build and refurbishment. A 1920s swimming pool was demolished to make way for the central cubic structure, composed of glass and the city's signature yellow stone, and designed by architects Nicholas Grimshaw and Partners.

At the top of the complex is the open-air pool. Below that is a floor with steam rooms containing fluted pillars around a central device where spa goers can walk into a mist of scented steam lit by state-of-the-art fiber optics. There are also treatment rooms, a gym for yoga and Pilates, and a big thermal pool at the bottom.

Healing claims for the waters persist. The Thermae Development Company, Dutch operators of the spa complex, state:

Sufferers [of all ailments], from sports injuries to rheumatic pains, sinus-related ailments to skin problems, will find healing properties in the spa waters. Bath's reopened spa, taking water from a very pure source, will be a relaxed, sociable environment contributing to the well-being of all users—a much-needed resource in today's very busy and very stressful world.

All the bathing facilities in the spa complex use natural spring water cooled to 91.5°F. Sand filtration, enhanced UV, and minimal chlorine dosing for residual disinfection are the only treatment requirements.

Whether you choose to align to the sacredness of this ancient place or not, the fact remains that it's once again active in the 21st century, a time when we need all the magic we can get.

○ ○ ○

NOTES

1. R. J. Stewart, *Waters of the Gap: Mythology of Aquae Sulis,* Bath: Bath City Council, 1981.

2. The article appeared in the Summer 1998 edition of *Kindred Spirit* magazine, issue 43.

3. Margaret seems to have succeeded in making the city council aware of the need for guardianship, as its Website now states that it's the guardian of the baths.

FURTHER INFORMATION

For more information on Thermae Bath Spa, go to: **www.bathspa.co.uk** or telephone (44) 1225 477051.

Kindred Spirit magazine: **www.kindredspirit.co.uk**

○ ○ ○   ○ ○ ○

CHAPTER 19

MOTHER GANGES, INDIA'S SACRED RIVER

by Elizabeth Puttick, Ph.D.

Verily, Ganga is the path to heaven of those that have bathed in her current.
— FROM THE *MAHABHARATA*

The story of the Ganges, from her source to the sea, from old times to new, is the story of India's civilization. . . .
— JAWAHARLAL NEHRU

SACRED WATER IN HINDUISM

Hinduism is the world's oldest religion, rooted in a reverence for nature and the interconnectedness of life that's largely missing in Western culture. In an animistic society, nature is alive with spirit—literally animated. Every rock, tree, and stream has its own spirit, which humans can perceive and communicate with. Oblations may be offered in return for blessings. Over time, in a development that Westerners call *polytheism,* the most important spirits became personified as gods and goddesses, with greater powers requiring more elaborate propitiation rituals. Water has been an object of worship from time immemorial, and among the most worshipped deities are Indra (king of heaven and god of rain), Varuna (god of water) and the river goddesses.

Over the last few millennia, Hinduism has evolved through

many different stages and manifestations, becoming more urbanized and "sophisticated," but nature gods and goddesses are still worshipped in the villages. Even in urban society, they remain vital spiritual and artistic forces.

For the purity-conscious Hindu social system, in which pollution is inevitably accumulated on a daily basis, water plays a central role in both domestic and public rituals. Water is a purifier, life giver, and destroyer of evil; it cleanses, washing away impurities and pollutants. In most Hindu families, it's considered auspicious to keep a vial of *Ganga jal* (sacred water from the Ganges) in the house. This is used to purify the body, household objects, and rooms. Bathing or sprinkling oneself with water is the customary way to rid oneself of impurities when entering the house, before eating, and on many other occasions.

Water is also important in rites of passage. Newborn babies are sprinkled with water in a ritual similar to Christian baptism [see Chapter 11]. Brides take a ceremonial bath similar to the Jewish *mikvah* [see Chapter 12], while the groom has his feet washed by his prospective brother-in-law. The last rite of life is to place drops of sacred water (preferably Ganga jal) in the dying person's mouth.

Water is also essential to temple ritual. Every temple has its own sacred wells and tanks, and both priests and worshippers bathe before entering the sanctum. Statues of the gods are immersed in water before installation; and daily libations of water, or flowers and leaves soaked in holy water, are offered to gods, *rishis* (saints), and ancestors. Water may also be sipped during prayers and invocations.

To Hindus, all water is sacred, but rivers are particularly venerated on account of the purifying quality of running water. Water absorbs pollution; but moving, flowing, or falling water has a great cleansing power that carries impurities away. This power can be utilized by sprinkling water over your head or taking a dip in a running stream—rituals that remove most kinds of daily contamination. The current of a river changes constantly, but in the body of the river dwells a spirit who controls the flow of the water. River spirits are propitiated and deified as goddesses.

GANGA MA: SACRED RIVER AND GODDESS

Map of the Ganges from source to sea

There are seven sacred rivers in India, of which the holiest is the River Ganges (Ganga). Its source is high up in the Himalayas—India's holiest mountains—in a glacial cave. For over 1,500 miles, it flows through the plains and cities of northeastern India, joining the sacred river Jumna (Yamuna) at Allahabad before eventually merging into the Bay of Bengal. Mythologically at least, the Ganges courses way beyond its earthly boundaries to the realm of *moksha*—spiritual liberation.

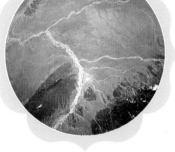

The Ganges has been held sacred for millennia and is repeatedly invoked in sacred Hindu texts, including the Vedas, Ramayana, and Mahabharata.

Satellite image of Ganges delta

In an ancient society that depended on the seasonal monsoons for its agricultural needs, the perennial nature of the Ganga was literally a godsend. Personified as *Ganga Ma*—Mother Ganges—the river is revered as a powerful goddess who embodies the cardinal virtue of purity, cleansing the sins of the faithful and aiding the dead on their path toward heaven:

Ganga is Righteousness in liquefied form. She is energy also running in a liquid form over the earth. . . . The very mother of the heavens, she has sprung from the highest mountain for running over the plains and conferring the most precious benefits on all creatures of the earth. She is the highest cause of all things; she is perfectly stainless. She is as subtle as Brahma.[1]

Ganga devi on lotus

There are many versions of the Ganges creation myth, but in most stories she transforms herself into a river and flows out of the big toe of the god Vishnu; or perhaps she manifests herself the hair (or ear) of the great god Shiva ("Salutations to Lord Shiva who holds Ganga in His matted hair"), or even the mouth of the silver cow Gomukhi. Ganga's heavenly origin and descent to Earth makes her an effective intermediary between the two worlds of humans and gods. Images of Ganga on a crocodile and Yamuna on a tortoise flanked the doorways of early temples. Entering the temple, devotees were symbolically cleansed by the purifying waters of these two rivers.

The Goddess Ganga seated on a crocodile

BATHING IN THE GANGES

In cities along the river, daily dips are an important ritual among the faithful. Many cities are considered sacred and have become pilgrimage sites for people from all over the world: Gangotri, at the river's source; Sagar Island, where it flows into the sea; Varanasi (formerly Benares), the holiest city of all, one of the world's major pilgrimage centers and the most auspicious place to die; and Allahabad, where the Ganga and Jamuna meet, the site of the most important festival in the Hindu religious calendar, *Kumbh Mela,* where millions of pilgrims from all over the globe gather for the bathing ritual.

Many Hindus believe that water from the Ganga can heal sickness of body and soul and cleanse the soul of all past karma. *Ganga jal* is often used to anoint the forehead of someone who's ill, and is drunk with one's last breath to take the soul to heaven. Even a single drop of Ganges water, carried by the wind over a great distance, is believed to cleanse a lifetime's sins. "By seeing, touching, and drinking the waters of Ganga, or even by applauding Ganga, hundreds and thousands of sinful men became cleansed of all their sins" (from the Mahabharata).

Ganges ghat

245

Bathing, immersion in the river itself, is even more purifying. Hindus may travel great distances to scatter the ashes of their relations in the waters of the Ganga, with the aim of helping them attain a better rebirth, and ultimately freedom altogether from samsara (the cycle of death and rebirth).

Even more desirable is to be cremated in Varanasi, the most sacred city on the Ganges: It's been said that "Death, which elsewhere is polluting, is here holy and auspicious." People travel from all over India and even internationally to spend their last days in Varanasi. The river is lined with ghats (stone platforms with steps leading to the water), where the funerals are held, and the pyres burn nonstop.

POLLUTION AND PURITY

There's a paradox at the heart of Hinduism, which reveres nature but isn't a "nature-loving" culture in the Western sense. Gardens and parks are often left untended, even in wealthy suburbs, and animals may be neglected or mistreated. Yet while mangy curs wander the streets looking for scraps, cows still have right of way and hold up the traffic with impunity. Plants may wither, unwatered under the burning sun, while flower garlands adorn honored guests and idols. The implications of this contrast between belief and practice have ironic and tragic consequences in the ritual use and abuse of India's sacred rivers.

As a mother, Ganga is tangible, accessible, and all-accepting: No one is denied her blessing. However, though her devotees revere her, they don't always treat her with the love and respect she deserves in return for her many blessings.

While the spiritual purity of the Ganges has remained unchallenged for millennia, her physical purity has deteriorated to the point where she has become one of the most polluted rivers on Earth. Many of the world's rivers are contaminated through human exploitation, but the Ganges has suffered particularly—partly as a consequence of what could be called "spiritual exploitation." Thousands of sick people with open wounds and festering ulcers bathe in the river daily to get healed, and these numbers swell into the millions during festivals, which also puts tremendous strain on the antiquated sewage system.

Dying in Varanasi takes the impurity out of death, but at the cost of putting pollution into the river. Some 40,000 cremations are performed there each year, and many more take place on other sites along the river. Most funerals are carried out on wood pyres that don't reduce the body to ashes; but the remains are thrown into the water regardless, to be fought over by dogs and vultures. The thousands more who can't afford cremation have their bodies simply thrown into the Ganges. It's an all-too-common sight to see partially burnt corpses floating down the river, along with the carcasses of thousands of dead sacred cows and assorted household rubbish.

Sacred ritual is only one source of pollution. The Sacred Land Film Project has produced a report on the Ganges, based on extensive scientific research, which identifies the main source of contamination as organic waste—sewage, trash, food, and human and animal remains. Around a billion liters of untreated raw sewage are dumped in the Ganges each day, along with massive amounts of agricultural chemicals (including DDT), industrial pollutants, and toxic chemical waste from the booming industries along the river. The level of pollution is now 10,000 percent higher than the government standard for safe river bathing (let alone drinking). One result of this situation is an increase in waterborne diseases, including cholera, hepatitis, typhoid, and amebic dysentery. An estimated 80 percent of all health problems and one-third of deaths in India are attributable to waterborne illnesses.

Wildlife is also under threat, particularly the river dolphins. They were one of the world's first protected species, given special status under the reign of Emperor Ashoka in the 3rd century B.C. They're now a critically endangered species, although protected once again by the Indian government (and internationally under the CITES convention). Their numbers have shrunk by 75 percent over the last 15 years, and they have become extinct in the main tributaries, mainly because of pollution and habitat degradation. However, at least in one stretch of the river, numbers are rising, owing to the efforts of the "Dolphin Man," Dr. Sandeep Behera from World Wildlife Fund India.

There have been various projects to clean up the Ganges and other rivers, led by the Indian government's Ganga Action Plan, launched in 1985 by Rajiv Gandhi, grandson of Jawaharlal Nehru. Its relative failure has been blamed on mismanagement, corruption, and technological mistakes, but also on lack of support from religious authorities. This may well be partly because the Brahmin priests are so invested in the idea of the Ganga's purity and afraid that admission of its pollution will undermine the central role of water in ritual, as well as their own authority. There are many temples along the river, conducting a brisk trade in ceremonies, including funerals, and sometimes also the sale of bottled Ganga jal. The more traditional Hindu priests still believe that blessing Ganga jal purifies it, although they're now a very small minority in view of the scale of the problem.

One famous environmental campaigner is Dr. Veer Bhadra Mishra, a Hindu priest who's also a civil engineer. He approaches pollution from both a scientific and a spiritual perspective, and has proposed an alternative sewage-treatment plan for Varanasi that's compatible with the climate and conditions of India. His "Clean Ganga" campaign is currently trying to persuade India's central government to adopt the plan, so far without success.

Dr. Mishra describes the importance of protecting this sacred river: "There is a saying that the Ganges grants us salvation. This culture will end if the people stop going to the river, and if the culture dies the tradition dies, and the faith dies." Mishra feels it important to find new language for the river that respects the Hindu worldview and veneration of the Ganges. To tell a Hindu that Ganga—goddess and mother—is "polluted" or "dirty" is an insult, suggesting that she's no longer sacred. Instead, it needs to be made clear that human action, not the holy river herself, is responsible: "We are allowing our mother to be defiled." This approach has stimulated grassroots involvement in the clean-up effort and is transforming the work for environmental preservation into a model for cultural and religious preservation as well.

A MIDDLE WAY: INTEGRATING SCIENCE AND SPIRITUALITY

It's unknown how many people have been healed by bathing in the Ganges. Clearly, it's hazardous, and drinking the water is even riskier, although most bottled Ganga jal is either strictly processed and filtered or issued with a warning not to drink it. My Indian guru used to mock the "credulous fools" who drank the water direct from the river, but many pilgrims—including some Westerners who might be expected to be smarter—gulp it down enthusiastically. As a result, they often contract hepatitis, typhoid, or cholera. There's a belief that Indians are less likely to get sick than Westerners on account of their faith, but the virological explanation is that they do become ill but manifest fewer symptoms because their bodies have suppressed the reaction.

On the other hand, there are stories of "miraculous" cures. It's hard for the rational, skeptical Western mind to believe that the power of the mind can overcome the effects of such an enormous range and volume of pollutants, although we know that the placebo effect has great potency. However, there have been some very persuasive experiments demonstrating the power of prayer and intention in healing, and it seems likely that the collective faith of so many millions of pilgrims could have a transformative therapeutic effect—both on the water and on the human body.

It would be interesting to conduct experiments on Ganges water in the footsteps of Dr. Emoto to determine how far blessing and thanking the water could alter its condition, both at sacred sites along the river and on bottled Ganga jal sold for ritual purposes. One exciting, radical implication of Dr. Emoto's findings is a democratization of the process of working with energy and bestowing blessings. His results indicate that any person with a pure heart and clear intention can trigger a transformative effect on water crystals, thus undermining the need for priestly ritual and intervention. If human consciousness can truly affect the structure of water—as the evidence clearly demonstrates—then we all have the power to heal, whether we're ordained or not.

I think it's important to find a middle way between the extremes of hard-nosed scientific materialism and ungrounded, gullible spirituality. Having lived in India for years, I've witnessed and experienced the literal ill effects of unclean water, which is a major risk to personal and public health. In my opinion, environmental campaigners like Veer Bhadra Mishra and Vandana Shiva and charities such as WaterAid, which save the lives and improve the health of millions of poor people, do more good—physically, environmentally, and spiritually—than businesses (including temples) peddling "holy water" at the "very small price" of $35 a bottle to wealthy pilgrims and tourists. I can't accept that a drop of Ganga jal cancels all your karmic debts. Attaining merit surely requires a more muscular effort—a more engaged spirituality.

I'd like to give the last word to Dr. Veer Bhadra Mishra, who has done so much to publicize the crisis, provide practical solutions, and integrate the opposing philosophies—and has been recognized on the United Nations Environmental Program's Global 500 Roll of Honor, as well as honored as a *Time* magazine "Hero of the Planet." For Mishra, the Ganga represents the meeting point where two worlds combine. He describes the world of scientific thought as being one bank of the river, and the deeply spiritual world, one alive with a limitless pantheon ("I would say there are as many gods and goddesses as people who live in India") as the other bank. And, he says, they're both equally important:

> We have to clean all the rivers, and only then our hearts will be happy. . . . It cannot be clean just by technology, just by setting up the right kind of infrastructure, there has to be an intermixing of culture, faith, science and technology. We have that kind of living relationship with the river. You [Western societies] have the best technology. So both the societies need to interact with each other to take care of these rivers.

○ ○ ○

NOTES

1. Quotations on the sanctity of the Ganges are taken from the Anusasana Parva, Section XXVI of the *Mahabharata,* translated by Sri Kisari Mohan Ganguli (**Indypublish.com**, 2004).

FURTHER READING

Kelly D. Alley, *On the Banks of the Ganga: When Wastewater Meets a Sacred River,* University of Michigan Press, 2002.

Stephen Alter, *Sacred Waters: A Pilgrimage up the Ganges River to the Source of Hindu Culture,* Harcourt, 2001.

Diana L. Eck, *Banaras: City of Light,* New York: Columbia University Press, 1999.

David Kinsley, *Hindu Goddesses,* Delhi, 1998.

Eric Newby, *Slowly down the Ganges,* Lonely Planet Publications, 1998.

WEBSITES

Friends of the Ganges, a San Francisco-based organization that helps Sankat Mochan in its clean-up efforts: **www.crabgrass. org/ganges**

Sacred Land Film Project: **www.sacredland.org/world_sites_ pages/Ganges.html**

Vandana Shiva interview: **www.pbs.org/now/transcript/ transcript_shiva.html**

Veer Bhadra Mishra interview: **www.coveringreligion. org/2006/04/22/wade_in_the_water_veer_bhadra.html**

CHAPTER 20

WATER, THE MOON, AND THE SOUND OF THE PLANETS

by Sayama

There's a strong interaction between water and the moon, which is very apparent in the phenomenon of tides. The gravitational pull of the moon exercises a similar effect on the human body, since as much as 70 percent of it is water.

This knowledge was gathered by ancient cultures and kept by some indigenous tribes, and has recently been rediscovered and scientifically supported by our modern high-tech civilization. We live in very interesting times, where the gap between intuitive perception on the one hand and rational realization on the other is starting to close.

In nearly all cultures, the moon embodies the feminine principle and is related to the emotional world and the human spirit. Because of this, it can be seen as a symbol of intuition and emotional perception. The sun, on the other hand, embodies its opposite, the masculine principle, and is the symbol of reason, intellect, and rational scientific realization. From these two complementary opposites, holistic perception comes into being. It takes place in the human heart, and it's nurtured and carried by love.

ALL IN EVERYTHING

We live in a universe in which all is mirrored in everything, and all is contained in everything. A single cell of the human body contains all the information about the whole of the body; and in turn the human body contains all the information about our planet, our solar system and, most likely, the entire universe. This holistic philosophy of life was already described more than 2,000 years ago in the words of the Chinese sage Lao-tzu: "One can know the whole world without having ever stepped out of one's door."

Another very beautiful metaphor about water can be found in the I Ching (The Book of Changes), in which water represents one of the eight primal energies. It's described as always flowing and filling out all places and hollows. It's not afraid of any current or waterfall and yet it always stays faithful to its original flowing character. In the Chinese tradition of the five elements—water, wood, fire, earth, and metal—each element is related to a specific organ, sense organ, and mental and emotional qualities, as well as colors and healing sounds. The element of water corresponds in this case to the color blue; the kidney and bladder; and the ear, with its sense of hearing.

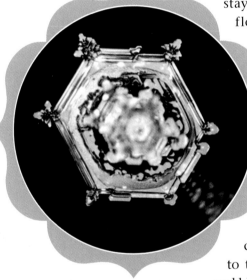

Water responding
to the color blue.

HEALING SOUNDS

At this point it's worth mentioning Masaru Emoto's water crystals and the vital role that water plays in our body. As the water crystals showed different reactions according to their exposure to sound, so our body, too, reacts directly to sound.

Music and sound therapy, which has become more and more popular in the past few years, uses this power purposefully and with positive results. Often the music comes from the traditional instruments of indigenous people or ancient cultures. Personally, I find that the most fascinating musical instruments in this context are the Tibetan sound bowls that originate in the Himalayas. These bowls are traditionally made of seven different metals, each vibrating at a different frequency.[1] Long ago, these metals were each assigned to a corresponding celestial body in the solar system:

- Gold: sun
- Silver: moon
- Mercury: Mercury
- Copper: Venus
- Iron: Mars
- Tin: Jupiter
- Lead: Saturn

Before being worked according to a formula that has been kept as secret as a precious recipe, each metal is placed for three days under the light of a full moon in order to absorb its energy.

The origin of the Tibetan sound bowls is lost in the mists of time, but they could date as far back as 7,000 years. It's believed that the Buddha used sound bowls some 2,600 years ago to accompany his meditation practice. Nowadays, they're still being played in Himalayan monasteries and in many parts of Asia to calm and clear the mind and focus thoughts and feelings during meditation, and also as an accompaniment during religious ceremonies. In the Western culture of the 20th and 21st centuries, they've found a place not just in music and sound therapy, but also in healing practices such as sound massage, sound journeys, and sound baths.

Playing the Tibetan sound bowls is quite easy. They produce a multilayered sound that's rich in overtones. Out of the interaction of many sound bowls, a range of attractive "soundscapes" comes into being, which harmonizes mind, body, and soul and opens up the heart. Experience has also shown that the bowls can balance the brain hemispheres and cleanse and revitalize the body's energy at the cellular level.

VIBRATIONS OF LIFE

Meditation practice supported by the sound bowls will enhance body-mind-spirit harmony in unison with the core principles of the universe.[2] How can we make the most of this wonderful realization and use it for health, well-being, and creative self-development?

The most beautiful and creative way would be to get a sound bowl and play it yourself, place it on your body, or feel its harmonious vibration in your aura. You can also experience the feel-good factor through a sound massage or a sound bath administered by somebody else. For most people, the easiest method is to make use of a CD.[3] That way you can have a sound massage or a sound bath any time you wish in familiar and comfortable surroundings just by lying between the speakers of a stereo system. In all of these methods, the body, mind, and spirit react immediately in harmony with the sounds; and the high percentage of water in our body starts to form beautiful crystalline structures.

I've also experimented with another method, which I use regularly because it has a very positive effect on me. I place a glass bottle of good spring water directly into a sound bowl (I recommend that you place a piece of cloth underneath the bottle so that no discord arises between the metal and glass), and I let the water absorb the vibrations for a few minutes. I choose a specific planetary sound according to whether I wish to go on a journey of self-discovery or initiate a healing process. Afterward, the water tastes softer and full of energy and, above all, absorbs the strength of the planet. I've experienced lovely results with these "planet essences." Their effect is similar to the Bach flower remedies—they're gentle yet powerful transformational tools and can be combined with other essences.

If you don't have a sound bowl at home, you can place the bottle of water between a stereo's speakers and let it absorb the vibrations. The CD *Chakra Sounds* features all 13 sounds of the solar planets and gives clear instruction as to how to manufacture your own planet essences.

Let's conclude by looking at water as an "information warehouse." When we drink water, we don't just take in fluids, but also the vibrations of life and nature, because water stores information throughout its infinite cycle. Spring water that's healthy contains "memories" of the leaves and blossoms on which it fell as rain, of the minerals and stones that it trickled through. It contains the vibration of the wind, the sea, the sun, and potentially the whole Earth's ecosystem. It reminds us of our origin and our evolution from a one-cell organism to a full-fledged human being.

Unfortunately, this is no longer true of tap water in most big cities. Because of various chemical treatments and the pressure inside the faucets, the water seems to lose its strength and information. Also, in recent times, more and more cell-phone transmitters have been erected on top of water towers and tanks. These have completely destroyed water's crystal structure, and the fluid has taken on artificial frequencies that are totally lacking in creativity. Luckily, however, thoughts and words such as *love* and *gratitude* have the power to neutralize those vibrations and "resuscitate" water's original attributes [see Chapter 7].

I've experimented with different methods: For example, sometimes I play nature sounds to tap water (rain, birds, the sound of rippling streams, and so forth) and then put the water in a jug with crystals (such as amethyst or rose quartz). Then I place the jug on a picture of a natural landscape—be it mountains, sea, or forest—to restore to this "sad" water its original information and vitality. The CD *Sacred Healing Waters* is ideal for this purpose, because water's journey from rain to spring to river to sea is set to music played on sound bowls, gongs, and bamboo flutes, which are mainly tuned to the sounds of the moon, the sun, Earth, and Venus.

○ ○ ○

NOTES

1. There are a number of different types of Tibetan bowls. When you play them, you can hear a variety of tones and overtones. All the notes can bring out similar vibrations in the body. You can place them around a person's body or on different chakras. This is like receiving a sound massage. As well as the seven different metals, there are also bowls made from quartz crystal. You can get a lot from recordings of these bowls, but nothing is like hearing them live. The different sounds affect different parts of your body—the sound "AA" impacts your heart, for example, while the sound "EE" vibrates in your head, around your pineal gland.

2. For those who wish to go more deeply into this topic, I recommend the CD *Chakra Sounds* and the book *Chakren im Wassermanzeitalter (Chakras in the Age of Aquarius).*

3. The Sayama CDs *Sacred Healing Waters* and *Sacred Healing Touch* (both available from **www.realmusic.com**) are recommended here because they've been produced mainly with sound bowls, gongs (tuned into planetary sounds), and nature sounds in excellent 24 bit, 96 kHz sound quality and therefore do justice to the sensitivity of the human ear. The majority of people who were muscle-tested (via kinesiology) for these CDs showed positive results.

○○○ ○○○

CHAPTER 21

RITUALS FOR CELEBRATING THE SACRED GIFT OF WATER

by Maril Crabtree

The sacred energies of water are a source of healing, guidance, inspiration, illumination, and spiritual wisdom for our life journeys—sometimes in marvelous and mystical ways. Water can be used to celebrate everything from the mundane to the extraordinary, alone or with a group, on holidays or any day.

To use the sacred energies of water in rituals and ceremonies, remember that everything in the energy realm begins with intention. Take a moment to align your intention with the cosmic consciousness—that space within and without where everything is interconnected. From that space, call in the sacred energies of water to assist you in accomplishing what you intend.

In my work as a hands-on energy healer and spiritual coach, the energy of intention plays an important role. Water becomes my ally; after every healing session I join my client in drinking water that carries its pure vibration to enhance the goals of the healing.

When you become aware of water's gifts, you can bring your intention to the water you use in your everyday life and create rituals for those uses. Most of us bathe or shower on a frequent basis. Why not pause just before turning on the shower or climbing into the bath and give thanks for this gift that cleanses, refreshes, and renews not only the body but also the mind and spirit? Take another moment to silently create whatever intention you wish— an intention for serenity as you go through your day, for example.

You'll then be ready to receive the benefits of water at a much deeper level as you immerse yourself in it.

Receiving the benefits of water can, in and of itself, be your intention as you go through your day. Whether you drink from a water fountain or your own bottle, be mindful as you sip. In your mind's eye, see the fluid hydrating and replenishing all the cells in your body. You can also carry an atomizer of water with you. When you feel stressed or upset, take a moment to spray the air just above your head and lift your face to receive the droplets of water. In doing so, you'll be giving a self-administered blessing to your body and spirit—and those around you will also be thankful!

We'll explore other examples below, but don't be afraid to create your own rituals to meet your desires and needs.

WATER FOR HEALING AND CLEANSING

Soft candlelight and music surrounded four women seated in comfortable chairs, their eyes closed, their bare feet in tubs of warm water, looks of bliss on their faces. Four other women sat, one in front of each partner, rhythmically cleansing, massaging, and applying lotions to the feet.

The women were participating in the ancient ritual of foot washing. They took their time with it. Each washer focused fully on the woman in front of her, giving her feet loving attention in complete silence.

"It was heavenly," one woman said afterward. "I was surprised that I enjoyed giving the foot washing as much as receiving it. After a while, my hands seemed to merge completely with the foot I was working on—I simply disappeared into it."

Others agreed. Before the ritual, we'd invoked the healing presence of water; and afterward we all felt relaxed, refreshed, and transformed in a way that connected us with more than hands and feet. Use this ceremony with your partner, your best friend, or a small group to enhance well-being for everyone.

One friend discovered that she had lung cancer and used water's healing gifts to help herself. Each day, after taking time to focus her intention, she drank water from a glass with the words *healed, whole, and grateful* taped to it. As she drank, she visualized the water going to the cancer cells and transforming them, then floating them out of her body. "The water tastes different," she said. "It becomes my ally in healing."

A woman with breast cancer used two water rituals. First, whenever she could, she went to the ocean and lay back in the water, arms open to signify that she embraced all the healing the universe had to offer. She visualized the sea flushing the cancer cells out of her body. Although natural water may feel better, you can do this ritual in a swimming pool, an indoor exercise pool, or even in your own bathtub. The important thing, again, is to align your intention and then create a strong vision of water flushing away those damaged cells.

This woman's second ritual involved other people. Inspired by Dr. Emoto's research, and knowing that the body is at least 70 percent water, she invited her friends to come and write positive affirmations on her camisoles and T-shirts. She also invited them to bring their own favorite pieces of clothing and write whatever messages of self-love they wished. In a rainbow of colors written with waterproof pens, the words *dance, celebrate life, sexy, love,* and *gratitude* graced her camisoles and T-shirts at the end of the evening. "Now, whenever I get dressed," she said, "I feel the healing power of those words lying next to my skin."

The healing benefits of water can bring a true sense of community by connecting and uniting those with a common purpose. In the midst of our women's circle sat a large crystal bowl filled with water. This water, our leader said, represented the tears of our sisters everywhere, and the loss of life and dignity women experience all over the world through being treated as less than equal.

One by one, each woman sat next to the bowl, speaking words of solidarity and support to their unknown, unseen sisters. As we spoke, many of us added our own tears to those in the bowl. At the end of the ceremony, we carried our sacred water outside and poured it into a nearby stream, adding it to the waters that nourish the earth.

WATER TO CELEBRATE LIFE PASSAGES

When Mark and Melissa fell in love, they felt like soul mates. They were so grateful for having found each other that they decided to marry at Thanksgiving and asked me to plan their wedding. A simple water ritual at the heart of the ceremony provided everyone with the opportunity to give the couple a special blessing. A large pitcher of water stood next to an empty bowl. One by one, friends spoke words of blessing, pouring water from the pitcher into the bowl as they did so.

At the end of the ritual, the bowl was filled with clear, sparkling water containing all the blessings. The couple poured some of the water into two goblets and, looking into each other's eyes, drank it, while I spoke of how these mingled blessings would strengthen their love. They took the rest of the water home with them, bottled some of it to freeze and drink on their first anniversary, and poured the remainder into the garden they'd planted together.

You can adapt this ceremony for births, bar mitzvahs, birthdays, graduations, memorial services, and other life transitions. Use it to create blessings and prayers for harmony, world peace, or for any other intention a group wishes to express.

CONNECTING WITH THE WHOLENESS OF WATER

Listen to the sounds of water: the whoosh of ocean tides, the tinkle of fountains, and the steady musical drip of gentle rain. Feel the liquid against your skin: smooth and silky or pounding and prickly, enveloping you in a womb of buoyancy. See how water sparkles in sunlight, how a rushing creek foams and curls against the stones, how a deep lake looks still and bottomless. Smell the ocean-salt tang, the brine of old rivers, and the fresh scent of waterfalls.

To celebrate water is to take pleasure in and honor its sounds and smells and textures and faces. Sift through your water memories: What stands out? Do you remember the first time you went into the ocean, bobbing joyfully and merging more and more with each wave? Perhaps someone gave you a dipperful of cold well water on a summer day. Did you revel in taking a long shower after walking several hours on a dusty trail? Have you watched a breathtaking waterfall as it cascaded down a cliff? What messages did you receive from your experiences with water? As you relive those memories with gratitude and appreciation, in the quiet of your room or in your own heart space, you're celebrating the sacred gift of water.

Anytime you want to experience the energy of that blessing, close your eyes. Picture that shimmering lake or those crashing ocean waves. Let their sounds and textures come alive for you. Soon you'll be floating in harmony with the universe.

Let sacred water be your guide and teacher to help you flow through life with the ease of a river, with the strength of a waterfall, and with the abundance of an ocean.

◌ ◌ ◌   ◌ ◌ ◌

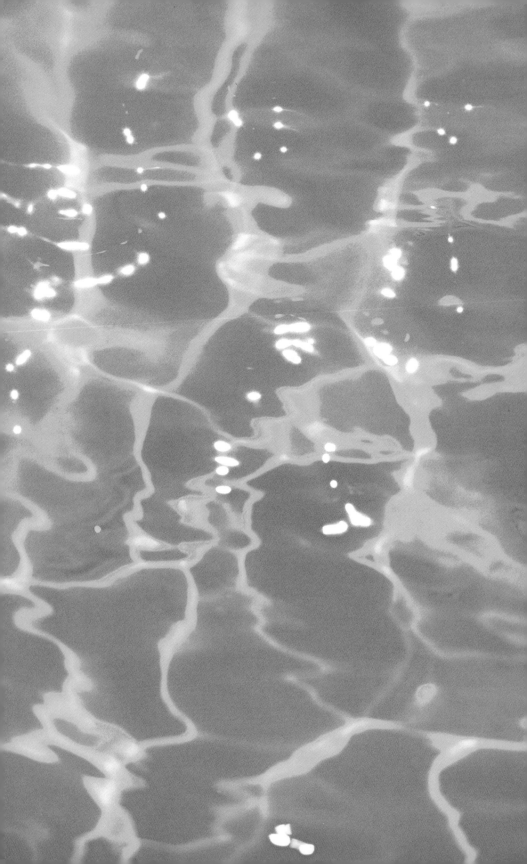

ABOUT THE AUTHOR

Masaru Emoto was born in Yokohama, Japan, in July 1943. He's a graduate of the Yokohama Municipal University's Department of Humanities and Sciences with a focus on international relations. In 1986, he established the IHM Corporation in Tokyo. In October of 1992, he received certification from the Open International University as a doctor of alternative medicine. Subsequently, he was introduced to the concept of micro-cluster water in the U.S., and Magnetic Resonance Analysis technology. The quest thus began to discover the mystery of water.

He undertook extensive research of water around the planet, not so much as a scientist, but more from the perspective of an original thinker. At length he realized that it was in the frozen crystal form that water showed us its true nature. He continues with this experimentation and has written a variety of well-received books in Japanese as well as the seminal *The Message from Water* (Volumes I, II, and III), published bilingually. He also wrote *The Hidden Messages in Water, The Healing Power of Water,* and *The True Power of Water.*

○○○ ○○○

About the
Contributors

MIRANDA ALCOTT

Miranda Alcott is a crisis responder, intuitive healer, and counselor who works with her service hearing/crisis intervention canine, Whisper. She has a master's degree in spiritual psychology and uses her awareness of energetic fields, colors, frequencies, and vibrations to help those who are confronting crisis in their lives.

RICHARD BEAUMONT

Richard Beaumont cofounded *Kindred Spirit* magazine in 1987 and has been its editor-in-chief for almost two decades. His investigations into the mind, body, and spirit have led him on countless investigations and resulted in him writing more than 100 articles. Recently he was on a live television broadcast of BBC4's *The World* program discussing the film *What the Bleep Do We Know!?*, which contains key references to Dr. Emoto's work. He has interviewed Dr. Emoto and filed several articles on the mysteries of water in the magazine. He's currently the director of the national organization for the dissemination of information on the Human Design System, which studies the genetic imprints behind incarnation. See **www.humandesign.info**.

WILLIAM BLOOM, PH.D.

William Bloom is one of the U.K.'s most experienced teachers, healers, and authors in the field of holistic development. His background includes a doctorate from the LSE, 2 years of spiritual retreat living amongst the Saharan Berbers in the High Atlas Mountains, 30 years on the faculty of the Findhorn Foundation, and being cofounder and director for 10 years of the Saint James's Church Alternatives program in London. He's a meditation master; and his books include the seminal *The Endorphin Effect* (Piatkus Books, 2001), *Working with Angels* (Piatkus Books, 1999), *Psychic Protection* (Piatkus Books, 1996) and most recently *Soulution: The Holistic Manifesto* (Hay House, 2004). He's currently heading up several projects to ground holistic spirituality into mainstream U.K. society. He lives in Glastonbury with his family.

PETRA BRACHT, M.D.

Petra Bracht is a physician who also works with natural remedies. She writes for a variety of medical journals and has published a book. She spent eight years lecturing on health and diet at the Johann-Wolfgang-Goethe University in Frankfurt and is currently a visiting lecturer. She appears regularly as a health expert on a variety of German television programs.

MARIL CRABTREE

Maril Crabtree is a writer, editor, energy healer, and spiritual coach. She's the editor of four anthologies of personal essays, meditations, and rituals on the impact of the four elements, including *Sacred Waters: Stories of Healing, Cleansing and Renewal* (Adams Media, 2005). You may contact her through her Website: **www.sacredfeathers.com**.

MAXIMILIAN GLAS

Maximilian Glas fell in love with stones at the age of ten and has been loyal to this love ever since. He studied mineralogy and became cofounder and editor-in-chief of the mineral journal *Lapis*. He has written numerous articles on the subject and organizes mineralogical exhibitions.

CARRIE JOST

Carrie Jost has been working with kinesiology since 1987. She has trained in many of the kinesiological approaches, psychotherapy, a variety of bodywork methods, and shamanic healing. She's currently head of the School of Creative Kinesiology in the UK, working with individuals and running training courses for practitioners who use kinesiology to help people find their way forward in life by dealing with the issues that get in the way. She brings her love of this work to everything she does.

DOLLY KNIGHT AND JONATHAN STROMBERG

Dolly Knight holds degrees in medicine and homeopathy and has cared for and helped many people and animals since the age of three. Jonathan Stromberg holds a bachelor of science in environmental geology and a master of science in engineering geology and is a fellow of the Geological Society. Together, they founded the Centre for Implosion Research in the UK in 1997. Both are members of the Scientific and Medical Network.

SIG LONEGREN

Sig Lonegren was taught to dowse over 45 years ago by his mother. He has a master's degree in the study of sacred space, is a past trustee of the American Society of Dowsers, and presently serves as vice president of the British Society of Dowsers and as a trustee at Chalice Well in Glastonbury. He's the author of three books on dowsing.

ELIZABETH PUTTICK, PH.D.

Elizabeth Puttick is a sociologist of religion and Indologist. She's the author of *Women in New Religion* (Macmillan/St. Martin's Press, 1997), numerous scholarly papers, and contributions to various books and encyclopedias on world religions, including the *Encyclopedia of Hinduism* (RoutledgeCurzon, 2007). Her spiritual path took her to India, where she traveled extensively and lived in an ashram for five years. Nowadays, she runs a literary agency in London (**www.puttick.com**).

RUSTUM ROY

Throughout his 60-year career, Rustum Roy has interwoven both world-class science and the reformation of theology and the practice of religion. He's at once a distinguished research scientist and a social activist, a societal reformer, and a champion of whole-person healing (or CAM). He currently holds professorships at Penn State, Arizona State, and the University of Arizona covering those fields. His work has been recognized by his election to five separate National Academies of Engineering/Science: the U.S., Sweden, India, Japan, and Russia. He has had the Order of the Rising Sun with Gold Rays conferred on him by the Emperor of Japan.

One of the key founders of the first major interdisciplinary field in the Western world's academia—materials research—he played the same role for the field of science, technology, and society. He has also been involved—usually as the only scientist—with cutting-edge reform of the Christian church. He has given the prestigious Hibbert Lectures in London and served on the Pope's Nova Spes Committee on Science and Religion, a field on which he has written and lectured for 50 years.

SAYAMA

"Sayama" Richard Hiebinger was born in 1964. He worked for several years in the field of music therapy with mentally handicapped children and for the last 15 years has been involved with sound therapy and holistic practices (Tai Chi, Qi Gong, meditation, energy work, and aromatherapy) to harmonize mind, body, and spirit with the aim of developing the human creative potential. He founded the record label Sayama-music in 1991 and has published numerous CDs, including *Sacred Healing Waters* and *Sacred Healing Touch* (both available from **www.realmusic.com**). His work is characterized by sensitive arrangements from different cultures of the world and by being in tune with the sounds of the planets as developed by H. Cousto. He regularly gives concerts and leads seminars.

RIVKAH SLONIM

Rivkah Slonim is the education director at the Chabad House Jewish Student Center in Binghamton, New York, and an internationally known teacher, lecturer, and activist. She travels widely, addressing the intersection of traditional Jewish observance and contemporary life, with a special focus on Jewish women in Jewish law and life. During the last two decades she has lectured in hundreds of locations across the United States and abroad, counseled individuals, and served as a consultant to educators and outreach professionals. She's the editor of *Total Immersion: A Mikvah Anthology* (Jason Aronson, 1996) and *Bread and Fire: Jewish Women Find God in the Everyday* (Urim, 200). She and her husband are the parents of nine children.

CYRIL W. SMITH

Cyril Smith was born in London in 1930 and worked on radar from 1947. He was a research fellow at Imperial College London in 1956, working on medical x-ray imaging. From 1964 until early retirement in 1989, he was lecturing at Salford University, where his research activities included instrument technology, medical electronics, dielectric liquids, and the electromagnetic effects in living systems and water. In 1973, he commenced his 18 years of cooperation with Herbert Fröhlich, FRS. In 1982, he began his involvement with the diagnosis and treatment of EM hypersensitive patients. He was secretary of the Dielectrics Society from 1972 to 1983. In 1990, his seminal book *Electromagnetic Man,* co-authored with Simon Best, was published. He continues to be active in research and writing.

STARHAWK

Starhawk is the author of ten books on Goddess religion, Earth-based spirituality, and activism, including *The Spiral Dance; The Fifth Sacred Thing;* and her latest, *The Earth Path* (HarperSanFrancisco). She teaches permaculture design with a focus on Earth-based spirituality, organizing, and activism in her Earth Activist Trainings. A committed activist for global justice and the environment, she travels globally, teaching, lecturing, and training.

JOSÉ LUIS STEVENS, PH.D.

José Luis Stevens is the president and cofounder (with Lena Stevens) of Power Path Seminars, an international school and consulting firm dedicated to the study and application of shamanism and indigenous wisdom to business and everyday life. He's based in Santa Fe, New Mexico.

José completed a ten-year apprenticeship with a Huichol *maracame* (shaman) in the sierras of central Mexico. In addition, he's studying intensively with Shipibo shamans in the Peruvian Amazon and with Pacos in the Andes in Peru.

He's a licensed psychotherapist, life coach, and teacher with more than 35 years of experience, and is the author of ten books and numerous articles, including *The Power Path* (New World Library, 2002), *Secrets of Shamanism* (Avon Books, 1988), and *Praying with Power* (Watkins, 2005).

WILLIAM A. TILLER, PH.D.

William A. Tiller, professor emeritus, Stanford University's department of material science and engineering and fellow to the American Academy for the Advancement of Science, is the discoverer of a second, unique level of physical reality—a new energy manifesting in nature. In his conventional science field, he has published more than 250 scientific papers, three books, and several patents. In parallel, for the past 30 years, he has been pursuing serious experimental and theoretical study of the field of psychoenergetics, which he thinks will become a very important part of "tomorrow's" physics. In this new area, he has published, to date, an additional 100 scientific papers and three seminal books: *Science and Human Transformation: Subtle Energies, Intentionality and Consciousness; Conscious Acts of Creation: The Emergence of a New Physics;* and *Some Science Adventures with Real Magic.* He currently directs the William A. Tiller Foundation for New Science in Arizona (**www.tiller.org**) and was a featured scientist in the movie *What the Bleep Do We Know!?*

DOREEN VIRTUE, PH.D.

Doreen Virtue is a fourth-generation metaphysician and clairvoyant doctor of psychology who works with the angelic, elemental, and ascended-master realms. Doreen is the author of numerous best-selling books and products, including the internationally best-selling *Healing with the Angels* book and card deck. She's been featured on *Oprah*, CNN, *Good Morning America,* and in newspapers and magazines worldwide.

Doreen teaches classes related to her books and frequently gives audience angel readings. For information on her products, workshops, message-board community, or to receive her free monthly e-newsletter, please visit: **www.angeltherapy.com**.

ALAN WALKER

Alan Walker is an Anglican priest and a lecturer in world religions for Florida State University (London Study Center). His publications include *Prayer for Everyday Living* (Godsfield Press, 2003) and *Vacations for the Spirit* (Godsfield Press, 2004). He's a regular contributor to BBC radio.

DR. DARREN R. WEISSMAN

Darren R. Weissman earned his bachelor of science degree in human biology at the University of Kansas and his doctor of chiropractic medicine degree at the National College of Chiropractic. He received additional intensive training in acupuncture, homeopathy, and other forms of energy medicine in Sri Lanka. Dr. Weissman's other postgraduate studies have included many other forms of energy healing. He's the developer of The LifeLine Technique, an advanced holistic system that discovers, releases, and interprets the root cause of physical symptoms and stress—emotions trapped within the subconscious mind. An internationally renowned lecturer, his mission is world peace through inner peace.

TERRI WINDLING

Terri Windling is a writer, painter, folklorist, and the director of the Endicott Studio for Mythic Arts (**www.endicott-studio. com**), an organization dedicated to creative arts inspired by myth, folklore, and fairy tales. She has published more than 40 books, including mythic novels (*The Wood Wife* and others), children's books (such as *The Winter Child*), and anthologies of magical fiction

(*The Green Man: Tales from the Mythic Forest* and more). Her articles on myth and mythic arts have appeared in numerous magazines, journals, and books, including *The Oxford Companion to Fairy Tales*. She has won seven World Fantasy Awards, the Mythopoeic Award, and the Bram Stoker Award; and she appeared on the short list for the Tiptree Award. Windling divides her time between Devon, England, and a winter retreat in the Arizona desert.

Hay House Titles of Related Interest

Crystal Therapy, by Doreen Virtue, Ph.D., and Judith Lukomski

The 8th Chakra, by Jude Currivan, Ph.D.

Energy Secrets, by Alla Svirinskaya

The Power of Infinite Love & Gratitude, by Dr. Darren R. Weissman

Practical Praying, by John Edward (book-with-CD)

Prayer and the Five Stages of Healing, by Ron Roth, Ph.D.

Secrets & Mysteries of the World, by Sylvia Browne

Secrets of the Lost Mode of Prayer, by Gregg Braden

The 7 Secrets of Sound Healing, by Jonathan Goldman (book-with-CD)

Silent Power, by Stuart Wilde (book-with-CD)

✿ ✿ ✿

All of the above are available at your local bookstore,
or may be ordered by contacting Hay House (see next page).

✿ ✿ ✿

We hope you enjoyed this Hay House book. If you'd like to receive a free catalog featuring additional Hay House books and products, or if you'd like information about the Hay Foundation, please contact:

Hay House, Inc.
P.O. Box 5100
Carlsbad, CA 92018-5100

(760) 431-7695 or (800) 654-5126
(760) 431-6948 (fax) or (800) 650-5115 (fax)
www.hayhouse.com® • www.hayfoundation.org

Published and distributed in Australia by:
Hay House Australia Pty. Ltd., 18/36 Ralph St., Alexandria NSW 2015
Phone: 612-9669-4299 • *Fax:* 612-9669-4144 • www.hayhouse.com.au

Published and distributed in the United Kingdom by:
Hay House UK, Ltd., 292B Kensal Rd., London W10 5BE
Phone: 44-20-8962-1230 • *Fax:* 44-20-8962-1239 • www.hayhouse.co.uk

Published and distributed in the Republic of South Africa by:
Hay House SA (Pty), Ltd., P.O. Box 990, Witkoppen 2068 • *Phone/Fax:*
27-11-467-8904 • orders@psdprom.co.za • www.hayhouse.co.za

Published in India by:
Hay House Publishers India, Muskaan Complex, Plot No. 3, B-2, Vasant
Kunj, New Delhi 110 070 • *Phone:* 91-11-4176-1620
Fax: 91-11-4176-1630 • www.hayhouse.co.in

Distributed in Canada by: Raincoast
9050 Shaughnessy St., Vancouver, B.C. V6P 6E5
Phone: (604) 323-7100 • *Fax:* (604) 323-2600 • www.raincoast.com

Tune in to **HayHouseRadio.com®** for the best in inspirational talk radio featuring top Hay House authors! And, sign up via the Hay House USA Website to receive the Hay House online newsletter and stay informed about what's going on with your favorite authors. You'll receive bimonthly announcements about Discounts and Offers, Special Events, Product Highlights, Free Excerpts, Giveaways, and more!
www.hayhouse.com®

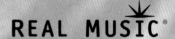

REAL MUSIC®

Sacred Healing Waters by sayama
(Featured in Chapter 20)

Sacred Healing Waters
by sayama

Sacred Healing Touch
by sayama

Soothing sounds of flowing water in harmony with bamboo flutes, Chinese harp, sound bowls and soft gongs to harmonize body, mind and spirit, allowing us to gently, gently let go.

800-398-7325
www.realmusic.com